THE
LIVING
JIGSAW

Male great spotted woodpecker

THE
LIVING
JIGSAW

The secret life in your garden

VAL BOURNE

with a foreword by **Chris Packham**
and photography by **Marianne Majerus**

Royal Botanic Gardens Kew

For my next generation,
India, Ellie, James and Jess

And for my postman Guy, often my
only point of contact with humanity!

© The Board of Trustees of the Royal Botanic Gardens, Kew, 2017

Foreword © Chris Packham 2017
Text © Val Bourne 2017
Illustrations © as stated in the acknowledgements on page 244

First published in 2017 by the Royal Botanic Gardens,
Kew, Richmond, Surrey, TW9 3AB, UK
www.kew.org

ISBN 978 1 84246 626 1

Distributed on behalf of the Royal Botanic Gardens, Kew
in North America by the University of Chicago Press,
1427 East 60th St, Chicago, IL 60637, USA

British Library Cataloguing in Publication Data
A catalogue record for this book is available from the British Library.

Editorial Development: Anna Mumford
Production Management: Andrew Illes
Design and page layout: Ocky Murray
Copyeditor: Brenda Updegraff
Proof reader: Matthew Seal
Indexer: Heather Robbins

For information or to purchase all Kew titles please visit shop.kew.org/kewbooksonline
or email publishing@kew.org

Kew's mission is to be the global resource in plant and fungal knowledge, and the world's
leading botanic garden.

Kew receives about half of its running costs from Government through the Department for
Environment, Food and Rural Affairs (Defra). All other funding needed to support Kew's vital
work comes from members, foundations, donors and commercial activities, including book sales.

Printed and bound in Malta by Melita Press

CONTENTS

FOREWORD BY
CHRIS PACKHAM

Hurrah! At last a gardening book that completely 'gets it'. A gardening book that begins by recounting a detailed observation and the intricate connectedness of a group of insects co-existing harmoniously on a white achillea – a gardening book based on actual ecology. A gardening book which sees a far greater beauty than can be made by just planting, weeding and mowing.

I've always struggled with aspects of gardening. I love the idea of using living things to sculpt an artificial environment, to personalise it. I've seen that as a real art and have always been able to appreciate beautiful gardens. But so often it seems to be achieved at the expense of tolerance and an understanding of nature. This leaves me wondering if it's about control, domination, the short term/ quick fix attitudes of our age and achieved at all costs, no matter how clumsy or destructive. Visits to garden centres where I've walked down aisles loaded with horrible arsenals of chemicals have deepened my mistrust of these superficial utopias. It seems as if gardeners fail to appreciate the inherent dynamism of life when it mixes in its inevitable complexity, and fail to realise that it cannot be forced, that the beauties forged by evolution cannot be twisted to fit or cancelled out for a convenience. So, impatient or unskilled, they resort to bullying and brutality and in a stroke, with a can, a spray or a powder, they wipe out the honesty of nature's harmony.

It's so heartening then to read this treatise designed to instil or enliven an interest in better, truer practices, to foster a deeper wrought ability to create dynamic, interesting, complementary assemblages of plants and animals and fungi which can genuinely be described as great gardens.

Chris Packham, New Forest 2016

A hummingbird hawk-moth

AN EARLY START

-1-
AN EARLY START

Like most gardeners I plough a lonely furrow, for whenever I have any spare time I head outside to tinker about. I've spent over 60 years doing just this, so my garden is my best friend, my solace, my exercise class and my inspiration. I caught the habit early from my grandmother, who was born in 1881, and I followed her hands-on methods – the same ones she had copied from her father before her. She was, of course, organic, although she never used that word or understood the concept. However, from the age of three I was inspired by her, and she taught me about the magic of plants. She had a tale about every plant and explained to me the joys of *Alchemilla mollis*, for instance, with its wonderful raindrop-catching foliage and jewelled edges, created when water seeps out round the extremities. I learned that it was named after alchemists who had thought the water magical and that it would be good for the complexion. She also explained why peonies could never be moved – in fact an old wives' tale, but it brought the garden to life and I soaked it up like a sponge.

My erliest memory is watching a bumblebee gather pollen and nectar from a frilly dark aquilegia at eye-level, so I have always been an insect watcher as well as a flower lover. In my mind they're completely integrated: the moving layer that hovers above the floral layer has always fascinated me just as much as the flowers. As for many people, my childhood garden fostered an interest in the natural world.

Some years ago I wrote a book called *The Natural Gardener* about the way I garden. It put forward the idea that it was quite possible to have a lovely garden without resorting to any chemical props. I wrote it because I have always gardened naturally and had lovely gardens. It didn't mean that I was immune to problems. I had slugs and snails just as much as

> ## GOLDEN RULE
> Engage your children and grandchildren: they are the next generation of guardians.

Clockwise from top left: Ellie picking
broad beans for supper; India supervising
from the wheelbarrow come seat; Jess picking
broad beans; pirate James about to pick dahlias

you probably do, and occasionally I sacrificed my runner bean plants or all my
cosmos to the hungry gastropod – leaving me muttering darkly for days. Most
of the time, though, my plants flourished and I rather took it for granted that
most people gardened like me, big-booting the slugs and snails when needed,
counting the ladybirds and chasing the bees.

When I began writing in 1995, spurred into action by recycled inaccuracies
penned by people who had plainly never picked up a garden fork, I was definitely
in my own gardening bubble. I landed a question-and-answer
slot on my local radio station. I was part of a team of four
and we popped up at random in pairs. The other three were
men and the pecking order relegated the 'newbie' lady to last
'dibs', so I picked up the crumbs after the 'main men' had
been given the question first. I was horrified by their answers
and I swear that steam came out of my headphones as I sat
there. The standard response to everything, whether it was
sooty mould on laburnum, black spot on roses, sickly lavender
under hedges, was to get a 'quick fix' from the garden centre.
They were recommending a chemical arsenal of things I'd
never heard of, let alone used. For the first time in my life I felt completely out
of kilter with the gardening world.

> *I had slugs and snails just as much as you probably do, and occasionally I sacrificed my runner bean plants or all my cosmos to the hungry gastropod – leaving me muttering darkly for days.*

My answers were off their Richter scale and my denouement came just a few
weeks later after I had the temerity to suggest that one caller bin her rose
because it was a martyr to black spot. 'Organic answers are of no use,' I was told,
so I resolved there and then to write a book championing my
natural gardening style. I had one major problem, though. I
had no idea why my garden functioned as well as it did.

The first thing I did was to analyse the questions I'd been
asked on *Dig It*, which I cynically renamed 'Spray It'. On
many occasions the caller's plant was simply in the wrong
place: there were straggly lavenders under shrubs and phloxes
with mildew in dry gardens. Plants were being expected to
grow in places where they were unhappy, but it was a problem
that could be easily remedied. Move the plant, or grow something else more
suited to the conditions.

GOLDEN RULE

Select the best plants possible and put them in the right place.

Sometimes the choice of plant was poor and there's no excuse for this. The Royal
Horticultural Society trials plants and gives the very best the Award of Garden
Merit (AGM). Trialling is thorough and judged by experts, and I've played my
part in this. Look for the trophy logo, or the initials AGM, because it is only

Choose your plants wisely and look for the AGM

given to the very best. Plants are like people: there are good eggs and 'wrong uns'. Don't waste time on the also-rans.

My choice of plants didn't wholly explain why my garden thrived, though, or why I had so few problems with pests and diseases. I spent five years frisking my plants and observing before I began to write *The Natural Gardener*, and by the time the book was published in 2004 the world had moved on. The EU Pesticides Review, which ran from 1992 until March 2009, had already led to many garden products being withdrawn or reformulated. This was largely due to expensive litigation following the use of chemicals such as Benlate, a fungicide that harmed unborn babies and our environment.

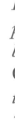

I spent five years frisking my plants and observing before I began to write **The Natural Gardener,** *and by the time the book was published in 2004 the world had moved on.*

As a result there were empty shelves in garden centres. Letters began to appear in worthy publications, such as the RHS *The Garden* magazine, decrying the fact that the chemical for pea moth, for instance, was no longer available. Many were indignant and took the attitude that they had been deprived of the means of keeping their individual plots in order, rather than looking over the wall and up to the sky to the planet beyond. Editors began to ask me to write articles about my own garden and how I managed it.

Things were happening on the conservation front too, because by the early years of the third millennium the decline in bees, birds, butterflies, wildflowers and insects had finally been acknowledged. The Bumblebee Conservation Trust was founded in 2006 by Professor Dave Goulson, then of Stirling University, and is still going great guns. However, native bees are just the tip of the iceberg. I knew the natural world was in decline, for I could remember cycling along Warwickshire lanes in the late 1960s and putting up clouds of butterflies feasting on hemp agrimony (*Eupatorium cannabinum*), or spitting out moths as the light failed at the same time as the lungs began to struggle too. That abundance has all gone, and that herald of spring, the cuckoo, so beloved of the British, has mostly disappeared, partly because these birds failed to find enough large moths to feast upon. A further reminder, as if I needed one, was re-watching a video shot in the mid-1990s in my Hook Norton garden – the garden that featured in *The Natural Gardener*. The garden is alive with insect life, little flecks of movement above the flowers. Twenty years on there's less of a buzz, less of a flutter and less birdsong.

> ## GOLDEN RULE
> Look at your garden as your part of the universe. Even small patches count.

Suddenly (and how my English teacher hated that word), gardens were seen as nature conservation sites. Garden-centre shelves, devoid of Derris Dust and all the other chemical paraphernalia, began to fill up with hedgehog homes, lacewing hotels and bee refuges – although the insects couldn't read the labels. My insects used dead stems, leaf-litter and long grass.

In 2005 I left Hook Norton after 18 years. The Best Beloved and I moved to a new garden at Spring Cottage. It was a weedy third of an acre plot devoid of any garden plants. Worse still, the garden shed was full of out-of-date chemicals that included, among other things, a yellow tin of DDT. It was straight down the snake and back to the start, with no ladder in sight.

You will encounter fewer problems in a chemical-free garden.

However, ten years on there's now a healthy ecosystem, drawn in by the planting and gardening style, and I've learned a lot more about how gardens work. This new book champions natural gardening, but goes much further. It says yes, you *can* do it, and you will encounter *fewer* problems in a chemical-free garden, not more. You'll enjoy it more, you'll be healthier and, most importantly of all, so will our planet.

Bees on deep-blue eryngium

Two small coppers on compact
Origanum vulgare 'Compactum'

A garden bumblebee (*Bombus hortorum*)
on species centaurea

Mating 7-spot ladybirds

CHAPTER 2

MY DAMASCENE MOMENT

-2-
MY DAMASCENE MOMENT

I started gardening at the age of three, so it seems fitting that my Damascene moment involved two small girls aged four and six. These two sisters, great-nieces of the Best Beloved, visited me in 1998 and immediately noticed a white achillea covered in blackfly by the garden gate. Questions hit me like arrows, thick and fast. What are those black things? Why are those ants going up and down the stem like that? What's that flying thing?

I'm not a scientist or an entomologist (oh how I wish I were), I'm just a gardener. However, I rose to the challenge and began to supply answers as efficiently as I could. I explained that the black things were blackfly (they were probably *Aphis fabae*) and that they had stylets (or feeding tubes) which they plunged into soft plant material. The sugary sap ran into their bodies, through osmotic pressure, and a sticky waste product called honeydew came out of their bottoms. 'Bottom' is a popular word with small children and I'm sure they giggled at this point. The sooty mould, so feared by gardeners, grows on the sugary, sticky honeydew. Unsightly, but not life-threatening!

Black ants (*Lasius niger*) were travelling up and down the stems to feed on the sugar-rich honeydew seeping out of the

> *'Bottom' is a popular word with small children and I'm sure they giggled at this point.*

aphids' behinds. They protect their food supply by farming the aphids and will see off any predators with their powerful jaws. They will remove the wings from any winged aphids, shield the aphids in bad weather and will carry them around to establish new colonies. Sometimes they take the aphids underground to their larder, never to be seen again. This type of cooperation is a bit like your granddaughter taking you shopping: she's going to be nice to you, ultra-nice, until she gets her heart's desire!

Whilst discussing all this sticky stuff, a small black creature landed in front of our eyes. The two girls assumed it was another blackfly because it looked so

Two hoverfly eggs on centaurea

A parasitic wasp, with wings, predating aphids on broad beans

A hoverfly egg and a clearly defined exit hole in a mummified aphid

similar in size. However, it was a parasitic wasp (*Aphidius*) and as we watched it bent its body over to form a comma, before placing one egg inside an unsuspecting aphid, using its ovipositor. 'What's it doing?' they asked. 'Well, that egg is going to grow inside the aphid whilst it's still alive and in seven days the aphid will become a brown blob because it's been mummified,' I replied. Their eyes widened. 'Fourteen days later the new parasitic wasp will emerge through the neatest round hole you've ever seen,' I said, and indeed we could already see some of these mummies with precision-cut holes, to illustrate this exodus. The new wasp will live for between 15 and 27 days and probably parasitise 200 aphids, as well as eating another 40 or more.

> *'What's it doing?' they asked. 'Well, that egg is going to grow inside the aphid whilst it's still alive and in seven days the aphid will become a brown blob because it's been mummified,' I replied.*

On other stems there were seven-spot adult ladybirds (*Coccinella 7-punctata*), feeding well away from the jaws of the 'yoyo' ants on their relentless march up and down. It was high summer and we could see seven-spot ladybird larvae feeding voraciously too.

Finally, thirst took over, so we retreated to the nearest seat and drank lemonade as we watched blue tits collecting more bounty from the old apple tree before flying on to their nest in the beech hedge. More questions followed, and I found myself explaining that a brood of blue tits needs to find 10,000 small creatures for their seven or so chicks in the three weeks before fledging. Bird seed won't do for most baby birds, I told them. They have to have tiny living things that wriggle.

As I explained these interactions to my still-rapt audience, describing things I've watched many a time in that garden, I found myself saying that all these creatures fit together like a living jigsaw. They all need each other to survive. And finally the penny dropped. I realised in a blinding flash, for the very first time, why my garden works. It's full of tiny interactions that allow these creatures to co-exist. They regulate each other. It's such a simple concept, once you've grasped it, and it makes much more sense than the garden mantra of good insect versus bad insect. It was the first time it occurred to me that this saint-and-sinner thinking was pie-in-the-sky claptrap. You need the full range of insects and you need to allow them to get on with it.

> *All these creatures fit together like a living jigsaw. They all need each other to survive.*

To use a simple model, the seven-spot ladybird feeds mainly on aphids and scale insects in order to survive. A sexually mature female seven-spot can lay 500 eggs throughout the summer. She lays batches of up to 50, always positioning her eggs close to aphid or scale insect colonies. The instars (or larvae) hatch from the oval, mustard-yellow eggs roughly four days later – all at the same time, in my experience – and consume their egg cases and any infertile eggs that haven't hatched. Darren J. Mann, writing in *Ladybirds*, says that tiny young instars ride piggyback on the aphids, although I haven't seen this – yet! As the instars develop, they shift from sucking aphid liquid to eating the entire insect, shedding their skins an average of four times before pupating. One instar will eat an average of 400 aphids or small insects in 35 days. A mature ladybird eats an average of 10 aphids per day. An adult will eat 5,000 whole aphids over its lifetime, according to the UK Ladybird Survey (also Rothamsted Research).

A sexually mature female seven-spot can lay 500 eggs throughout the summer. She lays batches of up to 50, always positioning her eggs close to aphid or scale insect colonies.

Between 10 and 35 days later, the larva pupates, forming an armadillo-like, orange-red pupa, which I often find on silver, woolly-leaved sub-shrubs such as ballota and phlomis. I also found them on the struts of my aluminium greenhouse – on the inside, though, where it was warm and dry. Two weeks later the new ladybird emerges, but the pigmentation takes time to develop. I have often seen pale, peachy ladybirds waiting for their spots and colour to develop, gradually turning from orange to red and black, rather like a newly emerged dragonfly waiting for its wings to harden.

This process takes several hours, but once their vivid black and red colouring is in place it's a warning signal to predators that says 'I'm not nice to eat, so don't bother.' When threatened, the ladybirds will secrete an alkaloid from their leg joints, and they also have smelly feet so when they visit a plant they leave a chemical trace. Rothamsted Research states: 'Parasitoids consistently avoid leaves which have ladybird "footprints" on them. This is because the ladybird leaves a chemical footprint when it walks across the surface of a leaf. The parasitoid uses these footprints to recognise that the ladybird is around and does not parasitise those

Parasitoids consistently avoid leaves which have ladybird "footprints" on them.

aphids – this also prevents parasitised aphids from being predated by ladybirds and allows the parasitoid and ladybird to work together to control pests.'

Spurred on by my 'living jigsaw' moment, my first quest was to track down ladybird eggs – which I had never seen. I knew 7-spots had mated in my garden that month – April 2003 – for I'd tried to take pictures. They were balanced on

Harlequin ladybird larva

16-spot larva eating an aphid!

14-spot ladybird larva and aphids

7-spot larva

Geum 'Gibson's Scarlet', a fabulously photogenic green background for a red-and-black insect, so I set up the camera and tripod. That camera made a small sound when the shutter moved (even on silent mode) and this prompted frantic action on the part of the busy male. Three rolls of film later – some 108 shots – I had five in-focus pictures. They mate for hours, gloriously so, but only once a year: tantric ladybird sex!

They mate for hours, gloriously so, but only once a year: tantric ladybird sex!

I hunted high and low for the eggs for some weeks and then, as I was getting dressed one morning, I noticed an aphid-ridden *Euphorbia characias* growing close to the window of my downstairs bedroom. Cradled in the cupped bracts were clusters of amber eggs. It was a eureka moment for me. They turned out to be ladybird eggs laid by a 7-spot ladybird and were inches away from aphids. Once I'd seen one batch I quickly noticed others. Rarely have I felt so triumphant. The natural world is all around you in your garden, but sometimes you have to search high and low.

Most gardeners panic at the sight of aphids, especially early in the year. They react to the sight of these fragile beings as if they were locusts about to rampage

Ladybird eggs

Mating 7-spot ladybirds

through the biblical wilderness, eating everything in their path. However, even the most catholic aphid found in British gardens, the peach-potato aphid (*Myzus persicae*), visits only 40 plant families out of 620. In other words, many aphids are relatively species-specific, not insects that devastate anything in their path. That grey American lupin aphid (*Macrosiphum albifrons*), which first arrived in the UK in 1981, will feed only on lupins and nothing else. There are also aphids specific to hellebores, beech, willow, cypress, apples and roses.

Many aphids are relatively species-specific, not insects that devastate anything in their path.

The common approach on seeing an aphid – encouraged for commercial profit in my opinion – is to spray with a systemic insecticide. This will see off your aphid, but it will also kill the ladybird and much else besides. The aphid will bounce back quickly because it's the master of quick reproduction. It could produce 40 generations per year in ideal conditions, and it doesn't even have to mate to do it. The babies are already in position, a process defined as parthenogenesis. Pippa Greenwood, a plant pathologist and gardening celebrity, likens the process to a series of Russian dolls. That's a good analogy and I wish I'd thought of it! It's said that one aphid can produce 80 nymphs (baby aphids) in a week.

Sara Redstone of the Royal Botanic Gardens, Kew, who generously read the manuscript of this book prior to publication, tells me that 'each of the many aphid species has its own lifecycle, but there are some features uniting nearly all of them. One feature most species share is that they are incredibly prolific. Wingless adult female aphids can produce 50 to 100 offspring. A newly born aphid becomes a reproducing adult within about a week and then can produce up to five offspring per day for up to 30 days. The French naturalist [René] Réaumur [writing] during the late 18th century calculated that if all the descendants of a single aphid survived during the summer and were arranged into a French military formation, four abreast, their line would extend for 27,950 miles, which exceeds the circumference of the Earth at the Equator!'

A newly born aphid becomes a reproducing adult within about a week and then can produce up to five offspring per day for up to 30 days.

Aphids are prolific and successful, and if their predators could bounce back at the same speed as the aphid, there wouldn't be a problem in our gardens. However, common garden predators have much longer lifecycles than pests, often producing only one or two generations per year, not 40. The 7-spot ladybird, for instance, mates once between late spring and early summer and then lays batches of eggs

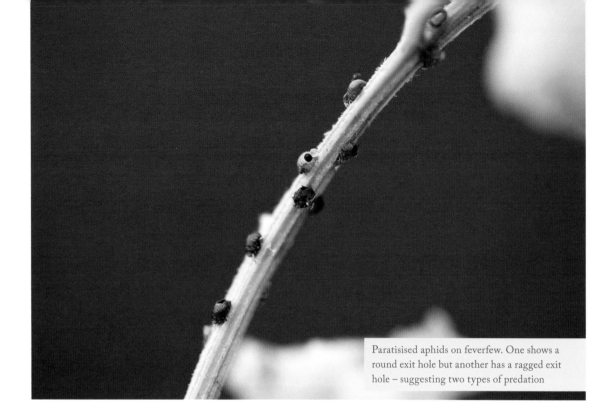

Paratisised aphids on feverfew. One shows a round exit hole but another has a ragged exit hole – suggesting two types of predation

close to aphid colonies. Spray in early spring and many adult ladybirds will die, meaning there will be very few around to help. Even if you get a new influx of 7-spot ladybirds, if they can't find any aphids in your garden they will have to move on. It's a catch-22 situation: no aphids means no ladybirds.

Without a full set of predators, you'll get more problems in your garden. Using green alternatives based on 'natural' products, such as garlic spray or soft soap, has the same effects. These controls may sound innocuous compared to an insecticide, but they will wreak the same ecological havoc on soft-bodied creatures and kill across the board. Much better to leave the aphids to your predators, or target them directly by rubbing them off with your fingers if they really offend you. Wear gloves if you're squeamish.

> *Using green alternatives, such as garlic spray and soft soap, still kill across the board.*

I know from first-hand experience how fragile aphids are. I found out in my early twenties when I worked in a lowly – very lowly – post at what was then called the National Vegetable Research Station (NVRS) at Wellesbourne in Warwickshire. Getting the job was a sheer fluke. I trained as a teacher, but couldn't get a position – probably because I wore micro-short skirts to every interview. However, my mini-skirt had an entirely different effect at the research station, which was full of young men at that time. I landed the job on my legs alone. Whilst there I worked in virology, and aphids were part of my remit because they transmit viruses as they feed on the plant sap. This is bad news for farmers and growers, so our job was to identify the virus.

Part of my time was spent trying to transfer aphids from infected plant material collected on the grower's land to healthy, large-leaved vector plants such as *Nicotiana* (tobacco). I had to look down a microscope and locate an aphid with a stylet, or feeding tube, plunged into plant material. I have to say that an aphid under a microscope is a thing of great beauty, perfectly formed. Then, armed with a fine paintbrush, I would tickle the aphid's rear end until it pulled out its stylet. At that point, I would deftly pick it up and place it on my new plant. This tricky process often ended badly, with dead aphids on the lab bench, minus their stylets. It taught me how vulnerable the aphid is, because time and time again the stylets would snap.

Armed with a fine paintbrush, I would tickle the aphid's rear end until it pulled out its stylet.

Our laboratory technique for farming more aphids involved using a non-systemic pesticide just once. I had to close up the greenhouse and remove the fine net covers from the plants and then spray. This killed most of the aphids along with most of the predators. The few aphids left bounced back thick and fast without many predators to devour them. Bingo: we had our supply of aphids.

In this lowly post I regularly lit nicotine cones in the greenhouse and dipped my fingers into a fungicide called Benlate. Benlate was banned in 1991, before the EU Pesticides Review got under way, because the American company who made it (DuPont) had been served with thousands of lawsuits. It cost the company $214 million to settle 220 lawsuits after Florida agriculture scientists claimed the product may have contained a potent chemical. In Florida, birth defects in the children of women who lived close to fields that had been sprayed with the pesticide were also discovered, including microphthalmia (undersized eyes) and coloboma (a defect in the structure of the eye). It's a grim reminder that human beings are at the end of the food chain.

With all this in mind, the sensible alternative in the garden is to leave your aphids alone and let your predators do the job for you. Garden birds will feed their fledglings on them, ladybird adults and larvae will frisk your plants. Hoverflies will lay their eggs and their larvae will devour the aphids. Lacewings will also join in the banquet. I look on my colonies of aphids kindly because they help other wildlife.

Red mites ring alarm bells with gardeners, but some predate aphids

Although I have a section in this book on birds (see page 79), it's worth mentioning here as well that lots of species of birds are in decline, and one of the main reasons is that their food supply has diminished. Long-term monitoring by the British

Trust for Ornithology (BTO) shows that starling numbers have fallen by 66 per cent in Britain since the mid-1970s. This led to the once common starling being red-listed as a bird in need of conservation action on the Birds of Conservation Concern 4 (BOCC4) Red List that is produced by the leading conservation organisations in the UK, although it is not red-listed by the International Union for the Conservation of Nature (IUCN). The cause of the decline in the UK is unknown, but starlings are heavily dependent on earthworms and leatherjackets, which have become less available perhaps due to there being less waste ground than in the past, more intensive farming and climate change.

> ## GOLDEN RULE
> Don't segregate your insects into saints and sinners. Look at them as part of a self-limiting food chain instead.

The cuckoo has suffered a similar fate. Since the early 1980s, cuckoo numbers have dropped by 65 per cent and, again, the reason is unclear. Decline in the populations of the main host birds – dunnock, meadow pipit, pied wagtail and reed warbler – has been suggested as a factor, as this would mean fewer nests available to the cuckoo to parasitise. However, the meadow pipit was the only host bird to have declined during the period examined by the BTO (1994–2007), so this would account for only about 1 per cent of the observed cuckoo decline. The cuckoo times its return from migration to coincide with the breeding cycle of its host birds, and it was thought that climate-induced shifts in the timing of breeding by these birds, of four to six days, could have reduced the number of nests available for cuckoos to parasitise. However, again this would account for only a small percentage of the decline, according to BTO research. The cuckoo is also on the BOCC4 Red List.

The cuckoo times its return from migration to coincide with the breeding cycle of its host birds.

The Royal Society for the Protection of Birds (RSPB) suspects that many migrants, including the cuckoo, are finding it increasingly difficult to feed themselves when they come to breed in Britain. Cuckoos eat larger moths and it's known that in recent years numbers of such insects have dropped significantly in the UK. There is also almost certainly a significant problem arising from climate change. When migrant birds arrive and breed, they have chicks at times which are no longer synchronised with the periods when food is most readily available.

The BTO recorded that the house sparrow has declined by nearly 71 per cent since 1977 and this bird is another red-listed on the BOCC4 list. Although the reasons for this in farmland habitats are well understood, the RSPB wanted

Once ubiquitous, the cuckoo is now a rarity

to discover what was happening to the birds in urban and suburban habitats. During 2003 and 2004 the BTO carried out an extensive field survey, building upon previous work and examining the relationship between house sparrow numbers and local habitat factors. The reduction in the availability of favoured food, for adults or chicks or both, was cited. It was noted that house sparrows are more abundant, and population declines lower, in socially deprived areas where there was more waste ground. Gardens tended to be less managed (in other words scruffier) and pesticide use was lower, so these areas provided more nesting sites and a greater abundance of food.

That last study reminded me of living next door to a 90-year-old lady in the wilds of Northamptonshire in the late 1970s. Too frail to garden, Mrs V's patch was an overgrown wilderness that wasn't popular in the village. However, we saw whitethroats, flycatchers and treecreepers right up until she died. Once the

The rural wasteland

garden was cleared and replaced by lawn, however, the birds went. This is why I believe every garden should have undisturbed areas built into their design, rather like the wildlife strips we now see on farms. Gardening should be far more than an exercise in neatness.

It's well documented that intensive agriculture has led to a decline in wildlife. In recent years there has been a U-turn with the introduction of grants for wildflower verges to help our birds, bees and butterflies. When I walk near home now, I see these strips of wildflowers and it is making a difference. There are more insects, wasps, beetles, spiders, hoverflies, bees and butterflies on my walks. This has meant more birdlife too. My grandchildren love beetles and bugs, and they have been able to find them on our walks since the wildflower strips appeared.

In short, there's never been a better time to manage your garden naturally, because we can make a difference. We don't have to deal with a monoculture, as farmers often do, and our plots are important because they join up with other plots to form a green tapestry. So it's a good time to take the giant leap of faith and begin to look at the bigger picture. It can be done, my garden proves it, and you will find you'll get fewer problems.

There's never been a better time to manage your garden naturally, because we can make a difference.

Witch hazels and oriental helleboves
straddle winter and spring

CHAPTER 3

THE MOVE TO SPRING COTTAGE

-3-
THE MOVE
TO SPRING COTTAGE

Moving house is traumatic, a life event to be avoided if at all possible, especially for gardeners who toil on their plots and spend a small fortune on their plants. However, I knew that the time had come to leave Hook Norton, after 18 years there, because the village I knew was being eroded by pavements, kerbs, street lights and new builds. The days when my daughters and a school friend were joined in their small tent by a muntjac deer, who casually walked up the garden and got caught in the guy ropes, had long gone. Rather than wake me in the small hours, my two hysterical teenagers and their friend ended the night in the back of our yellow estate car with their feet dangling out of the boot. The only evidence (and I was sceptical when first told) was a severely disrupted tent and surprisingly large, deep footprints.

When the time came, the jewel-box-rich September flower garden sold the house to the first people who saw it, before any details had even been printed. The Best Beloved and I had never owned a home together, but we had been house-hunting for several weeks – although it seemed much longer – because we could not agree on a suitable house that we both liked in a place we both wanted to live. We had, however, seen a pair of run-down adjoining cottages, overlooking sheep pasture and down a no-through lane. We put in an offer, but the cottages were withdrawn from the market within days, following the death of one of the trustees. When they came up for sale by auction that November, at the height of a housing boom, the Best Beloved sallied forth (without telling me I might add) and secured them.

Within seven days of the auction we found ourselves moving in, on 5 December 2005. It was a bleak midwinter day, made even bleaker when the removal men left at dusk, taking most of my immediate needs – including clean knickers. Spring Cottage, the habitable part of the building furthest away from the road, had been empty for four months, and left open for viewers just before the auction. They had

Spring Cottage, December 2005. The only thing in the garden was six line posts, one cottage peony and some *Alchemilla mollis*

chipped away at the plaster, lifted floorboards and tried to lever off one fireplace in a quest to discover more. It offered basic but adequate accommodation so, though most of my possessions ended up in store, the prospect of a jolly Christmas beckoned, and at least we had somewhere to live under the same roof, albeit a bit ramshackle.

It was a modest cottage, perfect for a modest pair. It had been in the same family for over 100 years, until Mary, who had lived there for all but a few weeks of her 80 or so years, lost her husband and moved up to the top end of village to be with her son. Mary's family had been wheelwrights and two different generations had occupied each of the two adjacent cottages. There were three front doors, with not a letterbox between them, and the south-facing third of an acre garden was surrounded by low stone walls patterned with red, ochre and black lichens that glowed in the low winter sunlight. The plot was completely devoid of garden plants, save for one cottage garden peony and some lady's mantle (*Alchemilla mollis*), but every weed known to man seemed to thrive and there were some buried bedsteads that had to be excavated.

The jackdaws, used to the garden being an empty playground, still reeled and played in the bright, frosty winter.

The jackdaws, used to the garden being an empty playground, still reeled and played in the bright, frosty winter of 2005/2006. Great spotted woodpeckers flaunted themselves in the bare ash tree beyond the wall and a drystone-waller chipped away in the neighbouring field right through the winter. In spring the jackdaws nested in the derelict cottage's chimney and in summer they devoured the leatherjacket grubs, marching over the lawn for hours on end, heads bent. On wet summer days the green woodpecker would arrive and bore into a large ant hill in the so-called lawn.

The deeds went back to 1880. However, a local village hall displayed an older map on which Spring Cottage was clearly marked, so the Best Beloved took himself off to the County Archive the very next day. A map of 1753 showed our cottage as the 'Hovel in the Waste', much to my amusement. It had been owned by a freeman named John Aston and 'waste' meant ground that wasn't cultivated, not what we imagine today. Strips of cultivation surrounded the low-slung cottage, for the immediate area is well served by springs and streams. Further south the fields, still known as 'Drygrounds', are just that.

Our soil at Spring Cottage is rich and dark and a spring that once serviced the Town Well, as it is rather grandly called, still gurgles out below the eastern boundary, flowing into a stream that descends into the Windrush Valley below. Water flows under part of the garden, but the cottage sits on a solid foundation

The view to the south-west

Frost-covered lichens on the stone walls

of stone, as we found out when renovation work started. Most of the woodland we can see has been planted recently, encouraged by grants. Older village residents recall the open vista stretching for miles, before the trees blocked it out. One old quarry near the church houses allotments, one of which is now ours.

We lie close to the Fosse Way, a Roman road that still runs between Exeter and Lincoln, and we have a Roman lavabo – a basin for washing hands – in our low stone wall, although Mary's husband, Bill, had filled it with cement. Apparently the Fosse once separated the population into the civilised, who lived to the east, and the savages, who inhabited the lands to the west. I am delighted to be one of the savages, perched on the high ground and subjected to bracing air on a daily basis. Local vicars were famous for their longevity, which they put down to the brisk atmosphere. Let's hope they're right.

The night skies are magnificent here, although some have wanted street lights in our spread-out village of 200 people.

Our village has two names, Aston Blank and Cold Aston, and the clue to its character lies in the latter. Our garden, which lies on the southerly edge of the village, is the most exposed, so we pay for our pastoral view over grazing sheep, because the south-westerlies rage up the Bristol Channel and keep on coming. On the plus side, the night skies are magnificent here, although some have wanted street lights in our spread-out village of 200 people. It is quiet and, like many a house-bound writer, I have a special relationship with my postman, Guy. Often he's the only person I see.

The shrill carder bee, once so common, is probably now the UK's rarest bee

The red-tailed bumble bee (*Bombus lapidarius*)

Owls hoot in August, and ravens croak like frogs in flight as they part the sky. And yet we get far fewer birds here than in my last garden in the centre of a large village containing lots of gardens. Contrary to popular opinion, the countryside is not full of wildlife now, and this is partly highlighted by a book we have on bumblebees, the *Field Guide to the Bumblebees of Great Britain and Ireland* by Mike Edwards and Michael Jenner. They point out that there is evidence to suggest that some of our most threatened species of bumblebee were so plentiful in the past that, up to the Second World War, entomologists rarely bothered to record their presence in their surveys of insects. If only they'd known.

> *Contrary to popular opinion, the countryside is not full of wildlife now.*

Edwards and Jenner cite the shrill carder bee (*Bombus sylvarum*), which was 'everywhere as usual' according to H. M. Hallett, who recorded bees in Pembrokeshire between 1928 and 1956. J. B. Free and C. G. Butler, writing on bumblebees in the *New Naturalist* series in 1959, also had personal experience of most of the bumblebee species in the British Isles. However, David V. Alford (writing in *Bumblebees*, 1975) was unable 'to give first-hand accounts for many of them'. The shrill carder bee was one of five species studied in the UK Biodiversity Action Plan (BAP) of the 1990s. The first field study took place in 1998. Although this bee used to be widespread and easily identified, alarmingly,

The buff-tailed bumblebee on willow catkins

We have lots of bees that we can't identify

Looking up the garden. Old-fashioned daffoldils and cowslips sustain early flying bees

Edwards and Jenner recorded that in 'six person-weeks of searching', only two worker bees were found.

The Bumblebee Conservation Trust now records the shrill carder bee as probably the UK's rarest bee, being found in only seven areas in southern England and Wales. These 'fragmented populations' are found in Kent, Essex, Somerset, Wiltshire, Gwent, Glamorgan and Pembrokeshire. The principal causes of decline are given as the loss of flower-rich meadows and the intensification of farming and grazing practices. The shrill carder bee emerges late and needs to be able to find nectar in September, relying on common knapweed (*Centaurea nigra*), red clover (*Trifolium pratense*), red bartsia (*Odontites vernus*) and hedge woundwort (*Stachys sylvatica*), all flowers with long corolla tubes.

The widespread use of herbicides and nitrogen-rich fertilisers has eroded our wildflower populations. The hay meadow, once the natural home of so much flora, is a rarity in farming now because the trend is for large fields cut for grass-rich silage. The sward is cut several times a year, so any wildflowers are cut well before they flower or set and

The Bumblebee Conservation Trust now records the shrill carder bee as very rare, being found in only seven areas in southern England and Wales.

shed their seeds. Ripping out hedges and planting right up to the edge of the field have also denied bumblebees vital nesting sites. Nectar alone is not going to sustain our native bees.

So, although Spring Cottage sounds and looks like a rural idyll, nature is not all around us. In fact, if you garden in an urban setting your garden is likely to have more wildlife than rural areas have. David Goode, writing in *Nature in Towns and Cities*, confirms that urban gardens and allotments offer a number of different habitats. He cites a tiny garden in Bath, 800 m (½ mile) south of the city centre, where the owners, both keen naturalists, have diligently recorded the species they have seen since 1991. Their list includes 44 species of bird, including the sparrowhawk, bullfinch, marsh tit and redpoll, as well as four species of warbler. Butterflies total 20 species, of which the white letter hairstreak is the most unusual. Scarlet and tiger moths occur, together with hummingbird hawk-moth, convolvulus and elephant hawk-moths. Other insects include speckled and oak bush crickets and seven species of bumblebee. Their small pond, built in 1998, has attracted seven common species of damselfly and dragonfly, along with frogs, toads and common and palmate newts.

So, although Spring Cottage sounds and looks like a rural idyll, nature is not all around us. In fact, if you garden in an urban setting your garden is likely to have more wildlife than rural areas have.

Bath has green corridors, with 'wedges of land' (to quote Goode) that extend towards the city centre. These areas include meadows, woodland and golf courses. The Widcombe Valley, just south of the railway station, has pony paddocks and hay meadows. A stream flowing through these leafy suburbs supports purple loosestrife (*Lythrum salicaria*), marsh marigold (*Caltha palustris*), figwort (*Scrophularia nodosa*) and horsetails (*Equisetum*), together with umbellifers such as hemlock water-dropwort (*Oenanthe crocata*), lesser water parsnip (*Berula erecta*) and fool's watercress (*Apium nodiflorum*). A pair of buzzards nests in one domestic garden.

Bath's Abbey Cemetery, one of the earliest Victorian cemeteries in the country, is now overgrown with a mixture of meadow and wasteland plants supporting 20 species of butterfly, grasshoppers and crickets. Lesser spotted woodpeckers, sparrow-sized birds I have not seen since the mid-1970s, are known to occur there and have been joined by ravens nesting in a tall Wellingtonia or giant redwood (*Sequoiadendron giganteum*). Roe and muntjac deer graze the rides in the evening and venture into local gardens.

I'm reminded of teaching in the mid-1980s and taking children on a mini-beast hunt. The school grounds, regularly manicured by a team of men whose main accessory was the strimmer, proved a barren disappointment to my class of excitable eight-year-olds. However, the graveyard round the town's church, which was never mowed, was a hive of activity in early summer. A haze of creatures, caught like flecks in the sunlight, danced before our eyes and lots of insects, including large beetles, could be seen. Birdsong serenaded us in our work.

Roughly 47 per cent of Greater London is green space, while 24 per cent is private, domestic garden land and 2.5 per cent is 'blue space' – rivers, canals and reservoirs.

The city of Bath also has parks, such as Prior Park, and extensive downs. Goode records that Combe Down has many old stone workings and these house one of the largest colonies of greater horseshoe bats, along with lesser horseshoe bats and other species. Bath is a World Heritage Site and much of the landscape around the city is managed by the National Trust, which works at providing public access whilst promoting nature conservation. This august body has said that it intends to concentrate on acquiring land, rather than buildings, and this is a commendable aim.

Many other cities and towns provide a variety of habitats as well. Within the framework of London, for instance, Greenspace Information for Greater London in 2015 recorded that roughly 47 per cent of Greater London is green space, while 24 per cent is private, domestic garden land and 2.5 per cent is 'blue space' – rivers, canals and reservoirs. If you include parks, golf courses, sports pitches, arable farmland, meadows and pastures, woodland and scrub, wasteland and acid grassland, the proportion rises to roughly 50 per cent of the land in the GLA. Other cities, including Edinburgh, Belfast, Oxford and Leicester, have gardens that account for around 25 per cent of the areas.

This clearly shows that gardens are important spaces – 22.7 million homes in the UK have them, some 87 per cent of households, forming a total land area of 4,330 sq. km (1,672 sq. miles). This, according to David Goode, is an area greater than the county of Suffolk. The average size of a garden is 190 sq. m (227 sq. yards), and the size and the age of the garden vary and influence the ecology. A garden laid out in the 1920s is likely to be of a good size

Gardens are important spaces – 22.7 million homes in the UK have them.

and to have mature trees. It will therefore have more species than a small modern garden, although both are important, however near a city they are.

Goode cites a study of Buckingham Palace Gardens, right in the heart of London, organised by the London Natural History Society in the late 1990s at the invitation of the then head gardener, Mark Lane. The survey, which took place mostly in 1996 and 1997, involved taxonomists from the Natural History Museum and the Royal Botanic Gardens, Kew. They recorded 322 species of wildflower in this relatively undisturbed garden, including marsh pennywort (*Hydrocotyle vulgaris*), which, according to Clive Stace in the *New Flora of the British Isles*, is 'locally common' although you would not expect to find it in the middle of London. Mycologists found 700 species of fungi, with two species new to science. In all, 39 lichens were also found, an improvement on the two recorded in the 1960s when the air was less clean. Also recorded were 2,160 species of insect and 207 other invertebrates, of which 112 were spiders, 227 beetles, 287 flies, 22 butterflies and over 600 moths. A quarter of the total species-list of UK butterflies and moths visited Buckingham Palace's garden, despite it being in the city centre. In addition, 30 species of bird breed there, a similar number to those recorded in London's large city squares and Royal Parks.

A quarter of the total species-list of UK butterflies and moths visited Buckingham Palace's garden, despite it being in the city centre.

If you need further persuasion about the value of urban gardens, a 30-year study of a Leicester town garden was compiled by Jennifer Owen between 1972 and 2002. Her first book, *The Ecology of a Garden*, published in 1991 at the halfway stage, recorded 1,782 species of animals and 422 species of plants. In

Adding a touch of the wild to your garden can make an enormous difference to your wildlife

Leave seed-heads in winter – don't put your entire garden to bed

2010 she rounded off her research with a much more readable book, *Wildlife of a Garden – a Thirty Year Study*. By then, 2,673 different species had been found in her 'neat, productive' plot. Among the daisies, buddleia and orderly lines of lettuce there were 474 plants, 1,997 insects, 138 other invertebrates (such as spiders and woodlice) and 64 vertebrates (including 54 species of birds) and seven mammals. Jennifer Owen trapped many of her creatures in malaise traps (tent-like mesh structures) or traps laid on the ground and this gave her a much greater chance of naming them. Being a respected academic herself, fellow specialists helped in identification.

Her conventional suburban garden in Humberstone, some 2½ miles north-east of Leicester city centre, was laid out in the 1920s and measured 730 sq. m (873 sq. yards). It contained mature trees, a well-trimmed lawn, neat and swept paths, colourful flowers, vegetable and herb beds, fruit bushes and an old apple tree, flowering and evergreen shrubs, conifers, a pond, a greenhouse and a compost heap. She planted many annuals to attract her insects and left unharvested brassicas to flower. She also allowed weeds to flower, including three lamiums species (*Lamium maculatum*, *L. purpureum* and *L. amplexicaule*), hogweed

(*Heracleum sphondylium*), rosebay willowherb (*Chamerion angustifolium*) and feverfew (*Tanacetum parthenium*). A keen gardener, she dead-headed to keep the supply of flowers going, preferring to plant single flowers rather than doubles. She actively selected late-summer and autumn flowers to extend the season.

> *Suburban gardens are 'extraordinarily rich habitats... private gardens taken together might reasonably be described as the UK's most important nature reserve'.*

There were berries for birds, fallen apples and seed-heads. Standing vegetation was left intact until after Christmas and pruning was kept to a minimum. The planting style was designed to be dense at ground level to encourage beetles. The overhead canopy was created by native trees such as poplar, birch and willow, with layers of planting underneath, and she described her style as luxuriant. She didn't, she explains, 'use pesticide or poison on any creature because I was interested in what shared the garden with me. I enjoyed it and I was not a vicious or overly tidy gardener, though my father, who was very much of the old school, used to walk around with his eyes averted.'

Jennifer Owen's study is proof that suburban gardens can be 'extraordinarily rich habitats', to use her words. She suggests that 'private gardens taken together might reasonably be described as the UK's most important nature reserve'. However, her 30-year study also revealed the decline in the numbers of moths, butterflies, hoverflies, ladybirds and bees, although beetles and solitary wasps bucked the trend and increased. She acknowledged the vagaries of the British climate, noting that the 1970s were a boom time for insect and garden life because 'the weather was more reliable and British farmers' quest for productivity had yet to reach its most chemically destructive'.

GOLDEN RULE

Gardens in cities and towns can be very wildlife-friendly, perhaps more so than many rural gardens.

Urban and suburban gardeners will also have one advantage over me – warmth. The ambient temperature of built-up areas is much higher, up to 7°C higher, than that in rural areas. My younger daughter's house backs on to a bread factory that gurgles and murmurs into the night in an Oxfordshire town. The extra warmth from the factory and the light from all the lamps have encouraged an abundance of wildlife, yet she is just yards away from her town centre.

The summer borders, in early June, provide plenty
of insect-rich flowers

CHAPTER 4

PLANTING UP SPRING COTTAGE

-4-
PLANTING UP SPRING COTTAGE

My new garden at Spring Cottage lies only 20 miles further west of my old plot in Hook Norton. However, they are poles apart in just about every respect. The Hook Norton garden was dry and stony because a band of ironstone ran beneath the soil, so planting anything was a pickaxe job. On a warm day the heat would beat upwards, as if there were a giant radiator underground, so it was warm and well-drained. Hook Norton is also in a rain shadow, sometimes getting an average of just 50 cm (20 in) of rain a year, because by the time the south-westerlies reached the village they had already dumped the rain on the south-western Cotswolds – typically Stroud.

The dry conditions and poor soil in my old Hook Norton garden restrained the growth of many plants, so it rarely, if ever, looked out of control. It relied heavily on silver and aromatic plants able to cope with the conditions, or on bulbous plants. There were wonderful stands of *Agapanthus* and *Dierama* in the gravel and wispy *Artemisia* fronds that looked like tiny puffs of smoke. However, it was impossible to grow peonies and most roses (although gallicas, rugosas and ramblers thrived), because most hated the arid conditions and thin soil.

In contrast, Spring Cottage has deep, fertile soil and parts of the garden are spring-fed from below so they never dry out. It was the perfect opportunity to grow peonies and roses because both need cold winter temperatures, deep soil and good light, so from the beginning I wanted to lead with a backbone of these two in the summer borders. However, most roses and peonies (more of which in Chapter 6, on the summer border) have double flowers and these petal-packed creations lack nectar and pollen, so they are definitely not insect-friendly. Double flowers also lack reproductive parts, so cannot set seeds. This is the reason that double flowers outlast the singles by miles. They look showier and most gardeners, including me, love them. It's perfectly acceptable to grow double flowers, but you must surround them with a sea of insect-friendly flowers to compensate for your chocolate-box doubles.

Peonies are a passion, but their double flowers
offer nothing to pollinators

Being an experienced gardener, I thought I would be able to predict what would grow well, so I planted some tried-and-tested 'bee-pleasers', including *Nepeta* 'Six Hill's Giant', a soft-blue catmint that's hardly ever out of flower. It had behaved

> *I thought I would be able to predict what would grow well.*

beautifully in the drier conditions of Hook Norton. However, at Spring Cottage it was floppy-stemmed and one plant quickly covered a metre of ground, smothering everything in its path. *Anthemis* 'Susanna Mitchell', a sprawling lemon-yellow daisy, did the same collapsing act. Although they were great plants in Hook Norton, as they are in most drier gardens, they failed here.

Choice forms of cornflower-like flowers such as *Centaurea* 'Jordy', with silvery foliage and dark flowers, were also too aggressive in the rich Spring Cottage soil. *Stemmacantha centauroides*, which can be a vision of loveliness with its mosque-shaped papery buds, died out in the first Spring Cottage winter. *Artemisia ludoviciana* was also too coarse and rampant, and the foliage and stems took on a dull patina rather than a silver sparkle.

I tried sea hollies or eryngiums too. They are architectural in form and the cone-shaped flowers are great bee and butterfly pleasers when the flowers are fresh. Each sea holly thimble consists of hundreds of tiny flowers, each with a nectary base. *E. giganteum* was a Hook Norton favourite with buff-tailed bumblebees. They hardly left them and, as the light faded, they used the silver bracts as hammocks. On many a summer's morning I emerged at dawn to see them resting in the silvery ruff of bracts, like sleepy children after a day out. This biennial sea holly, known as 'Miss Willmott's Ghost', produced a stainless-steel sculpture that branched and shone in the light in Hook Norton; however, the damper areas of Spring Cottage reduced it to a limp, grey-green affair. I have found places now, drier spots, where I can grow this and some silvers. I can accommodate them under the study window, at the front of the house, and on south-facing edges of the borders. I also grow the bluer forms (such as *E.* × *zabelii*). However, they are never going to be as crisp and prickly as they were in the dry garden I once had.

> *Gardening is always swings and roundabouts or snakes and ladders, whichever you prefer, and as character building as cross-country running in big knickers when you're a teenager at school.*

Gardening is always swings and roundabouts or snakes and ladders, whichever you prefer, and as character building as cross-country running in big knickers when you're a teenager at school. Incidentally, ours were bottle-green. Fifty years later I am still cringing at the thought of running down the High Street. On the

Veronica longifolia 'Marietta' with *Lychinis coronaria* 'Gardeners' World'

Rose 'Wildeve' supplemented by insect-friendly *Penstemon* ' Andenken an Friedrich Hahn'

Phloxes love this garden because most of the borders are fertile and moist

Eryngium giganteum needs careful placing in drier spots

The garden in early June, ten years on

upside, at Spring Cottage I have been able to grow phloxes, heleniums, peonies and *veronicastrum*, all plants that failed in the dry conditions of dear old 'Hookie'.

The lesson is clear. Every garden is different, but within that garden there are also differences. There are frost pockets, so in a new garden watch where the frost lingers. There are damp patches where weeds spring up more easily than anywhere else. There are wind-blown, exposed positions where leaves can shrivel to brown dust, but equally there are quiet corners that the wind seems to miss. There are hotspots too, where it is as dry as the Sahara, and dry shade, which is the most difficult combination of all. It takes a year or two to assess the differences, but the wait's worthwhile, and you won't get everything right first time.

So while the Best Beloved and I wrestled with the weeds, the bindweed, the couch grass and the ground elder, we looked at our plot carefully. By the end of the first year we knew where the cold spots were, which were exposed, which were most sheltered and which areas were sunniest and driest.

I had plenty of advice from friends, and it was suggested very early on that the sloping plot should be flattened by a digger and the walls raised to provide

GOLDEN RULE

Every garden is different. Get to know your plot and focus on the plants that will do well in your conditions.

Roses and honeysuckle spill over the low walls into the field beyond

privacy. This 'hemmed-in' world would never do for me. I wanted to see across the fields and feel the big sky setting, because the Cotswold plateau stretches for 2 or 3 miles to the south-west. I wanted roses to spill over the waist-high south-facing wall, so that walkers stopped and stared, and I wanted the garden to merge into the meadow beyond the wall. After all, I had only one third of an acre. The slope stayed, along with the low walls, and we worked with it.

The borders follow the gentle incline upwards from the road, rather than cutting across it, so the eye travels up the garden as you walk up the front path. The seating area at the farthest end of the cottage is lower than the garden, so it's possible to peek through the flowers and hide away. Further privacy is provided by a wooden summer house and this gives scale to the exuberant autumn planting, which tends to be tall and impressive. The convex lawn, a third of the way up the slope, is still there and blue self-heal (*Prunella vulgaris*) still sprouts in July, delighting us and the bees, just as it always has. The six wooden line posts were a conundrum: they stayed for three years before I decided whether or not they had to go. They were concreted in – Bill's handiwork again – and proved a real trial once the decision was made to remove five of them.

> *Every garden is different, but within that garden there are also differences.*

I'm no garden designer, but a friend from Oxford, Sarah Naybour, is. She pointed out that Spring Cottage was a long, low rectangle and made the suggestion that the main borders should reflect this shape to give a balance between house and garden. This has worked well, and some of the garden flowers mimic the local flora. Hardy geraniums, clematis and scabious appear regularly, especially in the summer borders.

The Best Beloved and I also wanted fruit and vegetables, because organic gardeners tend to grow their own food. There had to be a spring garden, a summer garden and an autumn flourish, because my gardens have to offer something throughout the year. The lowest fifth of the garden was partly shaded by several large beech trees, to the north and south of the house, although they do not belong to us. It seemed best to site the woodland garden at the lowest end for this reason, although it has proved slightly too damp for smaller bulbs. As a result the snowdrops have had to march up the garden to drier ground, but the wood anemones have compensated. They adore the cool, damp soil down there. If I had my time again, the woodland garden might well have been at the higher, western end where drainage is better. Hindsight can be so annoying.

> *If I had my time again, the woodland garden might well have been at the higher, western end where drainage is better. Hindsight can be so annoying.*

Vegetables and fruit are also very important in the Spring Cottage garden

The summer garden runs along the front of the cottage, where it is sunny and sheltered, but the soil is very moist in parts because of the spring coursing underneath. These rose, phlox and peony borders peak in June and July, but they are extended into autumn by penstemons, cosmos and *Gaura*, so it's quite possible to have flowers lingering on until early November. The autumn finale is tucked on to the south-to-south-westerly edge so that fading sunsets catch the tall grasses and seed-heads as they move and sway. These three main areas are dealt with in detail in later chapters.

Provision was also made for long grass, in the shape of two bulb lawns, although sadly I couldn't find room for a pond. On the southern edge, there's a wilder area that is rarely disturbed, tucked up against the south-facing wall. It's a flourish of roses and honeysuckle in high summer, but it's impossible to prevent ground elder and bindweed, which reside under the wall, from creeping in too.

DIVERSITY IS KEY

I've found the crucial thing in gardening naturally is diversity, planting as many different types of plants as possible. I discovered this more through luck than judgement, because I'm a self-confessed plantaholic. I see it. I like it. I buy it and I plant it, shoe-horning it in before the Best Beloved returns and asks me where I am going to put it. As a result of my addiction, my gardens are diverse: they are packed with lots of different types of plants.

I discovered the importance of diversity when I began to think about *The Natural Gardener* for the first time around 1998. I began to look at insects and focused on the ladybird, because it was an easy starting point for someone without any entomological training: they're distinctive and easy to see. I counted the species in my Hook Norton garden and found five, just by looking carefully. Jennifer Owen, owner of the Leicestershire garden I mentioned in Chapter 3, noted one more species, but she trapped her ladybirds in order to count them. I spent a long time peering into plants with aphid colonies.

> ## GOLDEN RULE
> Embrace diversity and plant a range to include trees, shrubs, perennials, annuals, bulbs, grasses and ferns etc.

My ladybirds were all in slightly different places. I saw the 2-spot ladybird (*Adalia 2-punctata*) eating aphids on roses and I found hibernating two-spots near the shed and in the shed. The ubiquitous 7-spot ladybird (*Coccinella 7-punctata*) was usually seen on herbaceous plants, and it often hibernated close to the ground on plants with a winter presence, such as pulmonarias and ferns,

PLANTING STRATEGIES FOR A SUCCESSFUL, SUSTAINABLE GARDEN

- Identify your microclimates, because every part of your garden differs.

- Grow what will do well and put your plants in the correct place so that they are happy. Move them if they're not, or ditch them!

- Have a supply of flowers for as much of the year as you can: they will sustain pollinators by providing nectar and pollen. And remember, flowering trees and shrubs can be an invaluable source of pollen and nectar for insects – and often on a much larger scale than herbaceous plants.

- Focus on early-flowering plants. These are essential for solitary bees and bumblebees emerging from hibernation. Find a sheltered area for these, preferably one that gets afternoon sunshine, so that nectar flows in the cool days of late winter and early spring.

- Late flowers are equally important for late-flying pollinators.

- Leave some undisturbed areas on the boundaries.

- Mix your flower shapes so that you are growing as many different forms as possible – from daisy to umbel, from tube to saucer, and flat-headed landing stage. Mix the colours too. Different shapes suit different insects, and colour also matters. Bees love blue, flies prefer green and white.

- Plant densely. Pack plants together to create a leafy over-storey that will act as a mulch, preserving moisture and creating the perfect conditions for beetles – great predators of slugs. Do not separate each plant with a ring of soil: it's akin to crossing the Sahara if you're a ground beetle.

- Plant diversely. Make sure that you have trees, shrubs, evergreens, perennials, annuals, ferns, grasses and bulbs, because different plants shelter and sustain different creatures.

- Allow some of your lawn to grow into a long sward.

or in leaf-litter. They also liked conifer trees and *Leylandii* hedges. The ten-spot ladybird (*Adalia 10-punctata*) was often on the beech hedge that ran down one side of the Hook Norton garden, especially during an explosion of beech aphid. It will hibernate in leaf-litter, plant debris, beech nuts, bark, on tree trunks and in ivy, and can produce two generations per year. The 14-spot ladybird (*Propylea 14-punctata*), a creamy-yellow ladybird with 14 squarish spots often fused together, was also in the Hook Norton garden. It hibernated at ground level in leaf-litter, plant debris, grassy tussocks and plant stems, often clustered in large groups.

My last ladybird, the 22-spot (*Psyllobora 22-punctata*) is a yellow ladybird with 22 round black spots that don't join up. It feeds on mildew, not aphids, and is usually found close to the ground. It hibernates in long grass and this is where I saw it, in the small bulb lawn. The wide range of plants and habitats in the garden had attracted five species of ladybird.

RIGHT PLANT, RIGHT PLACE

'The key thing about building a successful self-sustaining ecosystem is to put your plants in the right place, then they will thrive without stress and avoid diseases. Don't slavishly follow an obsession for growing thirsty plants such as phloxes, New York asters and astilbes unless you have good, fertile soil that holds moisture and a garden that gets sufficient rainfall. If your garden, like mine, is cold, open, exposed and mainly damp, avoid most silver-leaved plants, or find that dry spot under a wall. You can't grow everything successfully, that's just life.

Mix the flower shapes and colours

A chilly dawn on a frosty day in winter can look lovely

CHAPTER 5

WINTER INTO SPRING

-5-
WINTER INTO SPRING

If I was carried up into the air whilst wearing a blue gingham dress and a crisply starched apron, like Dorothy in *The Wizard of Oz*, the one bit of garden I'd like to be sucked up into the vortex with me is the spring garden, for it engages my spirit more than any other area. When it's cold and grey, and the days are at their bleakest, I can see promise all around me and this never fails to excite me.

It starts early. By Christmas Eve, when the days are already lengthening, I may have some flowers of the miniature daffodil *Narcissus* 'Cedric Morris' out. The neat yellow flowers, which show lots of green on their backs, hunch up against the cold, a bit like me in my overcoat, muffled up against the weather. Or I may have an early snowdrop or two, such as *Galanthus plicatus* 'Three Ships', usually the first to follow the midwinter solstice. This squat little fellow has wide leaves, slightly pleated back at the edges, and clean white flowers with a seersucker ripple to the petals. There may even be a jaunty pink flower from *Cyclamen coum* if I'm lucky, perhaps supported by rounded silver foliage. These 'down on the ground' flowers, framed by bare earth, mean the world to me, for they signify that the year has turned. Spring is on its way.

On bleak days, when there are few flowers, I can satisfy myself by looking at the fists of snuff-brown buds on the ten or so witch hazels (*Hamamelis*) I've planted – almost certainly too close together. The buds are visible from autumn onwards, so you know whether winter's going to be glorious long before it is. Or I can focus on the wintersweet (*Chimonanthus praecox*), which may be showing a glimmer of pallid yellow within its satin buds. Or there might be a tiny glint of pink on the winter-flowering *Daphne bholua*, which always flowers in the first few weeks of the year. They will all please me just as much as anything pushing through the ground, for the garden is waiting to return and the anticipation is pure, stomach-churning pleasure, like waiting for a well-loved visitor to arrive.

On bleak days, when there are few flowers, I can satisfy myself by looking at the fists of snuff-brown buds on the ten or so witch hazels.

A glorious jumble of flower appears by late March

Witch hazel (*Hamamelis × intermedia* 'Harry')
lighting up the woodland garden in January

EARLY BEGINNINGS –
THE UNDERSTOREY

This was the first area I planted up, because when I left Hook Norton I took my prized hellebores and snowdrops – quite legally, I might add. I dug them up in late November, or as many as time allowed, and planted them some ten days later into freshly cleared ground. A frosty, bright winter followed and in the spring they all flowered successfully. However, my hellebores are a jumble of colour because it was impossible to know which was which.

I had also rescued some *Crocus* 'Vanguard' and a cardamine that had crept in with a hellebore. *Cardamine quinquefolia* bears mauve-purple flowers above five-fingered foliage, hence the name. The relief was palpable when my treasures flowered: they had survived the move and they seemed to say I would too.

Hybrid hellebores (*Helleborus* × *hybridus*) are still the main player in the spring garden and I've added more, of course. They have been acquired from good breeders such as John Massey of Ashwood Nurseries, or Hugh Nunn, raiser of the Harvington strain. Some go back further to Elizabeth Strangman's Washfield and Robin White's Blackthorn nurseries, both sadly gone now. Buy your hellebores in flower, because there are singles, doubles and semi-doubles in many shades. The flowers, which have sepals rather than petals, last for two months or more and buff-tailed queen bumblebees rely on them when they emerge from hibernation. On a warmish winter afternoon, they hover over them like 'Heavy Henry' Hercules cargo planes as they consider where to land.

Hellebores are prone to a fungal leaf spot disease (*Microsphaeropsis hellebori* syn. *Coniothyrium hellebori*), which makes dark patches on the foliage. Being organic, I won't spray them with a fungicide, but in early December the foliage is cut away to prevent this fungal disease from taking hold. Removing the leaves prevents mice from using the foliage as an umbrella and cropping off the flower buds when hunger takes over, a very annoying mousey habit. The hellebore foliage goes into the green waste recycling bin, even if it looks healthy. Then a slow-release fertiliser is sprinkled round them, because hellebores are greedy feeders. When they finally perform, the flowers stand alone, before the new foliage emerges, and look better for it. I always dead-head after flowering to try to prevent unwanted seedlings from draining my prized plants. Inevitably I do get seedlings, and these may stay or go depending on their position and my mood!

Hellebores are prone to a fungal leaf spot disease, which makes dark patches on the foliage.

Hellebore 'Anna's Red' glows in winter light

My hellebore collection is not appreciated by all. Nurseryman Bob Brown of Cotswold Garden Flowers frowned when he came to the garden and commented that there are 'too many hellebores, Val,' in the same superior tone adopted by Christopher Lloyd, who called us 'helle-bores'. No matter, for the bees adore them and the flowers last a long time, so they are good garden value, although nectar and pollen do dry up within the first few weeks. Avoid the dull pinks, though, which look drab and dreary, and always place the sooty-black hellebores carefully so that they don't get lost against the brown soil. They work against a backdrop of green, or close to a gleaming, pale birch trunk. One of the best colours in the garden is bright red and I've recently planted a hybrid called 'Anna's Red', which is a glorious, rich, ruby-red colour with frosted foliage. The apple-greens and whites stand out well in the garden, but yellows can be tricky because they are precocious flowerers and often catch the frost.

One of the best colours in the garden is bright red and I've recently planted a hybrid hellebore called 'Anna's Red', which is a glorious, rich, ruby-red colour with frosted foliage.

I've also planted lots of interesting small-flowered primroses because they enjoy the damp, cool conditions. They are great bee plants and they cross-breed easily because the arrangement of the stamens and stigma changes from the

A galligaskin primrose with leaf-like sepals

Wood anemones love this garden. Here *Anemone nemorosa* 'Robinsoniana' makes a large carpet

pin-eyed (with prominent stigma) to the thrum-eyed (with prominent stamens). Bees searching for nectar take the pollen from plant to plant without really trying. Over the years I've collected some interesting forms with hose-in-hose flowers, or a 'Jack in the pulpit' ruff of foliage underneath the petals, or the galligaskin forms with petals and leaves that are neither one thing nor the other. 'Barnhavens and Cowichans' – American primroses bred by Florence Bellis of the Barnhaven Nursery in Oregon – add much to the gene pool because she raised rich reds, amethysts and deep blues. I weed out the ordinary folk, then watch and wait to see the variety of colours and flower forms the bee has provided. The Best Beloved mutters darkly about 'introgression' affecting the local, native cowslips (*Primula veris*), but you can't please everyone all the time.

By April there are carpets of wood anemones, mainly named forms of *Anemone nemorosa*, but these self-seed and almost certainly hybridise. They form vast blocks, out-competing the snowdrops, because they thrive in this damp, cool area of the garden. Wood anemones are gently nodding flowers, often in milky colours, and they should not be confused with

The wood anemone often has darker backs to its petals and these are very visible in low light levels when the flowers hover between open and closed.

the flat-topped, multi-rayed and brighter *Anemone blanda*. The wood anemone often has darker backs to its petals and these are very visible in low light levels when the flowers hover between open and closed. I admire 'Robinsoniana' and 'Allenii', both darker-backed soft blues. The double white 'Vestal' is later, but very pristine. Hepaticas, such close relatives of the wood anemone that they once shared the name 'anemone', also thrive here. 'Harvington Beauty' is stunning, with cornflower-blue flowers.

THE OVERHEAD CANOPY

Planting up this spring border taught me a valuable lesson, for when the hellebores and snowdrops flowered in our first spring of 2006, the whole area looked like a bad-taste multi-coloured carpet. Early flowers, without a woodland canopy overhead, are a visual flop. They need trees to give all-important scale and to cast a magic-lantern pattern of light and shade. Their benign presence makes the soil drier and warmer, draining off excess moisture, and the overhead branches protect from the harshness of winter weather.

I would stand there, one sock up and one down, wondering how a tree managed to flower on such a grey, inhospitable day.

I began by ordering an autumn-flowering cherry – *Prunus × subhirtella* 'Autumnalis' – and it arrived as a small bare-root tree, which I duly planted. Even that one stick-like addition helped visually, although I chose it for nostalgia's sake. It was a tree of my childhood and I can clearly remember the blossom scudding over my grey primary-school playground. I would stand there, one sock up and one down, wondering how a tree managed to flower on such a grey, inhospitable day, before deciding which petal to scamper after. Autumn-flowering cherries, as they are called, thrive in London where I grew up. However, the cold Cotswold climate just about spares mine, so it will never be glorious here. Ten years on, it's still stick-like with a parasol top, mimicking its Japanese heritage, for most Japanese ladies of a certain age seem wedded to their parasols. It flowers in the clement patches between November and March, and there is something very magical and Harry Potter-ish about flowers on bare spidery branches, especially when they have a confetti-like quality.

I've added three more cherries to the spring garden. *Prunus* 'Kursar' flowers in early March in most years, the almond-pink blossom emerging from downward-facing buds on an open-branching tree. In autumn the foliage turns a pleasing orange, although I grow this cherry for its seductive pink boughs of blossom held against the spring sky. 'Kursar', raised by the famous breeder Captain Collingwood 'Cherry' Ingram, was once thought to be a hybrid between *Prunus nipponica* var.

Wood anemones thrive here

kurilensis × *P. sargentii*, hence the name 'Kursar'. Apparently it isn't, but in warm years the buds are a winter feature from January onwards and the dark branches look seductive in low light. Like all pink-flowered trees, it flatters deep, plummy hellebores. I also grow the Japanese apricot, *Prunus mume* 'Beni-chidori', for its single rose-madder pink blossom in March, and the shrub-like *Prunus incisa* 'Kojo-no-mai' – a March- or April-flowering, compact Fuji cherry with clusters of tiny white flowers held in bright-pink calices. All are very popular with the bees and some years they all flower together. One day I hope that the branches will stretch out their fingers and touch.

WINTER-FLOWERING SHRUBS

I have also planted ten witch hazels (*Hamamelis* × *intermedia*), purely for the joy they bring. These are fragrant, although their fragrance varies from freesia (as in 'Aurora' and 'Pallida'), to medicine-like 'Diane', to strong 'bathroom cleaner' through to almost nothing. Some of the showiest flowers hardly smell at all, but that's life – you can never have it all. If you want to plant for fragrance, smell them before you buy them. If you just want visual stimulation, please plant 'Aphrodite' – this brightly coloured witch hazel will ignite any garden. It's a good idea to buy witch hazels in flower during January, but do keep the pot in a sheltered position away from heavy rain and frost, for example in the lea of the house, before planting in spring.

Every winter I get marmalade strands in spicy orange, yellow and red running through the woodland patch, hopefully picked up by winter sun.

My deep soil suits witch hazels. They always flower in January and the flowers do not get damaged and browned by the cold weather. I have seen them survive heavy snow, severe frost, driving rain and searing winds without a hint of browning. So every winter I get marmalade strands in spicy orange, yellow and red running through the woodland patch, hopefully picked up by winter sun. Their splaying branches shelter diminutive woodlanders that include snowdrops, blue *Scilla siberica* and tiny narcissi. I would get bigger witch hazel flowers if I watered them in dry summer weather, when they slant their foliage down to almost vertical to avoid transpiration. These are, after all, plants that enjoy an Asian summer of warmth and heavy rainfall, so they will not do well in dry gardens or on thin soil. I rarely water anything, though, once it's established, because I feel it's a waste of resources.

I can rely on my witch hazels to be weather-proof, but winter-flowering daphnes and viburnums are vulnerable to the weather. They either hold back their flowers, or they brown in the slightest frost. *Viburnum × bodnantense* 'Dawn', for instance, a large pink-flowered shrub suitable for a boundary, is superb in November – wafting out a hyacinth scent when little else is flowering. Honeybees are often still about if it's mild, so it's invaluable in November, surely the bleakest month of all. It will continue to flower in mild patches up until April, although clusters of flowers brown if it turns cold. I also grow the March- and April-flowering *V. × juddii*. It's easy, has a good branching shape, and the white flowers on this semi-evergreen shrub are highly scented. They usually arrive in late spring; however, in mild years the flowers are earlier.

The trees and shrubs in the woodland garden are gradually growing to provide an overhead canopy

Even in my cold garden, wintersweet (*Chimonanthus praecox*) packs a powerful punch, and it's wonderful in a vase

FRAGRANCE

When everything is still and the sun is out on a clement January day I can get a waft of witch hazel perfume from afar, but mostly I have to sidle up close. I can't, by the way, bear to pick any of the branches! However, one winter shrub from China, wintersweet (*Chimonanthus praecox*), overwhelms you with fragrance even on the coolest day, and it lasts well in a vase too. It's the salve that soothes my winter blues, but there's a price to pay, for this large shrub is a Jekyll and Hyde character. Though lovely in winter, when the translucent, pallid-yellow flowers show their tomato-red middles, once in leaf it's uninspiring to put it kindly. It used to be thought tender and was usually grown against a warm wall, so I planted it in hope and expectation rather than certainty. However, it has thrived and shrugged off freezing winters in an open, exposed spot.

> *This large shrub is a Jekyll and Hyde character. Though lovely in winter, when the translucent, pallid-yellow flowers show their tomato-red middles, once in leaf it's uninspiring to put it kindly.*

A few feet away there's also a winter-flowering, shrubby honeysuckle, *Lonicera × purpusii*, and this is temperature-dependent. In a warmish winter it can be in flower at Christmas, producing downward-facing cream blooms that are highly scented. I have seen honeybees visiting it over the festive period, but in colder years it will flower as the foliage develops. It too is untidy in leaf, but the winter flowers are worth it.

Winter-flowering daphnes are rare, but *Daphne bholua* does oblige. Most selections were collected in the wilds of Nepal in the second half of the 20th century. They are variable, with deciduous and semi-evergreen forms, and generally the deciduous forms are collected higher up the mountains and are therefore hardier. Some have evocative names such as 'Gurkha' and 'Darjeeling'. The most garden-worthy is a seedling from 'Ghurka' discovered by Alan Postill at the Hillier Nursery in 1982. It has luxurious green foliage and clusters of pink flowers with an exceptionally sweet fragrance, and he very sensibly named it after his wife, 'Jacqueline Postill'. Daphnes are as good for bees as they are for hedonists.

I planted three 'Jacqueline Postill' and, of the three, one has survived unscathed by the weather. The other two were cut down badly and are trying to recover to become the columnar, 2 m (6 ft) tall daphnes they once were. Bearing this in mind, give 'Jacqueline Postill' a sheltered position, although all daphnes are notoriously capricious and can fade away without any reason during a single season. I have a garden rule that says when all daphnes are at their most glorious, plant another. 'Jacqueline Postill' usually begins to flower in January, but goes on until late March, and in the second half of spring the scent can be overwhelming.

If you've never grown a daphne, the easiest is *D. odora* 'Aureomarginata', although it will not flower until 'spring proper' arrives. It makes a wide, spreading plant and the mostly green leaves are not gaudily variegated. Instead they have a tasteful narrow rim of creamy yellow, irregular, but still nattily neat. The scent is glorious, although it will be a spring sensation rather than a winter one. I grow another purely for its high-gloss rosettes of evergreen foliage, *D. laureola*. This is our native spurge laurel, and the lime-green flowers are merely honey-scented compared to the intoxicating mixture of lily and carnation, my own interpretation of true daphne scent. The bees like *D. laureola*, a poor man's *D. pontica*, and it berries and produces some seedlings, although not too many. It's in a dank spot, but it doesn't mind, and that's where it grows in the woods near my home, in deep, dark shade. *D. laureola* is more luxuriant than Christmas box (*Sarcococca confusa*), for which the garden may be a little cold. It does in the woodland border, just about, but would be happier in a pot against the house.

> ## GOLDEN RULE
> ---
> **Early flowers are vital for bumblebees and solitary bees because, when they emerge, they need nectar for flight and protein-rich pollen for successful breeding.**

CONTINUING THE SHOW

I like this area of the garden to go on flowering into April and May, and it is damp and sheltered enough to grow North American trilliums and erythroniums. *Erythronium californicum* 'White Beauty' has the most handsome, with mottled foliage that gives this genus the name of trout lily. The warm shades of chestnut-brown on the leaves pick up the colour of the anthers exactly and, on a bright day, it's possible to see this brown necklace through the cream-white pagoda flower. Their success or failure depends on good spring rain, and in a dry, cool spring all erythroniums look miserable. I like to site them near forms of the soft shield fern, *Polystichum setiferum*, because the new russet-bristled fronds flatter the brown mottled foliage of 'White Beauty'.

The bees enjoy my erythroniums, but I'm not sure about the trilliums. Some have a meaty smell designed to attract small flies rather than bees. My most successful, *Trillium kurabayashii*, performs in March, when the deep-red petals form an upright cockade above the mid-green foliage, which is often heavily

Erythronium californicum 'White Beauty' has cream-white flowers held above mottled foliage

shaded in maroon-brown. Trilliums are very variable in the wild and I have some lovely forms of *T. kurabayashii*, so do try to acquire a plant in flower. This one will stay in leaf for months, although I've tucked my trilliums away in the most sheltered spot where the soil is still rich and moist. It took me five years to find a suitable place and I've added lots more, some grown from seed to flowering plant. This was a seven-year process and I felt as though I'd given birth, such was my joy. *T. kurabayashii* sounds oriental, but it's found in coastal areas of south-western Oregon and the lower slopes of the Sierra Nevada mountains in the United States. It was named after the Japanese botanist who identified it as a separate species and the name has been confusing gardeners like me ever since.

I have many trilliums, but the hardest for me is *T. grandiflorum*, because it emerges late here and is therefore more prone to being dried up by the sun. The canopy above is a walnut tree on the other side of the wall, which comes into leaf far too late to shade this later-flowering trillium. Perennial honesty (*Lunaria rediviva*) is another star performer here, with highly fragrant lavender flowers. I love the way it grows in stature, eventually reaching waist-height and throwing out odd flowers into summer after the main event. The oval seedpods rarely contain seed, sadly, because I'd like more. It's not grown nearly enough.

> *I love the way it grows in stature, eventually reaching waist-height and throwing out odd flowers into summer after the main event.*

The second battalion of woodlanders also includes a tall white catchfly that wanders a little even in drier shade. The white flowers are pinked round the edges, giving it the name of *Silene fimbriata*. It's one of the few white flowers I grow, along with the green-and-white striped *Tulipa* 'Spring Green' and white astrantias, which are always veined and tipped in green.

Ferns are another plant passion of mine and the wintergreen ones offer shelter to hibernating insects. Among the stars are forms of the soft-shield

Trillium kurabayashii needs shelter and fertile soil

fern, *Polystichum setiferum*, that include 'Bevis' and its sporeling 'Green Lace', raised by micro-propagation. There are neat, toothed forms like 'Herrenhausen' and densely mossy ones such as 'Plumosomultilobum' (syn. 'Plumosum Densum').

There are *Dryopteris* too, but their fronds become ragged at the turn of the year, so they are cut back to reveal dark-brown knuckles. The new fronds will appear in early May, coinciding with the English bluebells, and nothing catches the spring growth surge as much as an unfurling fiddle-backed dryopteris frond in spring. By far the best is a dark-black form, *D. wallichiana*, but this is variable and widespread in geographical range. Only the Himalayan form has handsome black hairs, so buy one you can actually see.

THE LAST FLOURISH

Green gets more soothing when the weather's warm, and I'm happy with a border that's mainly green and leafy in summer, especially because it's already delighted me for four months of the year. However, it's always worth extending the flowering season in any border beyond the main flourish if you can, so I have added some late-flowering *Hydrangea paniculata*. I began with the cool white-green 'Limelight' and progressed to the subtler white lacecap 'Kyushu', which is highly popular with insects. These have a hard time, because they are pruned back in early December so that their branches don't spoil the snowdrop show. I have avoided the large and brash ones, such as 'Phantom' and 'Vanille Fraise', but they are superb under enormous trees and all will flower in dark shade.

> *It's always worth extending the flowering season in any border beyond the main flourish if you can.*

Ferns major in the spring border. Here *Polystichum setiferum* 'Ray Smith' extends its fronds like a starfish

The waxy pink flowers of *Daphne bholua* 'Jacqueline Postill' scent January afternoons

Viburnum × bodnantense 'Dawn' flowers whenever the weather allows

By the end of May all the colour has disappeared, leaving a green tapestry

High summer here is glorious

CHAPTER 6

THE SUMMER BORDER

-6-
THE SUMMER BORDER

These are the blocky borders closest to the cottage, so, in order to avoid the bare-earth look in winter, there are regularly spaced box balls that carry the eye up the garden when everything else has retreated underground. That way pleasure can be gained from the view through the window when gardening vicariously on inclement winter days. Somehow those glistening box balls lessen the frustration of not being able to go outside.

In summer the box balls are barely visible amongst the summer froth, which is a good thing, because they are not as regular as I would like. I grew each one from cuttings taken in 2005, because box blight, *Cylindrocladium buxicola*, seemed to be ravaging nursery stock at that time. I rather wish I'd planted ready-formed ones, for the box leaves are not consistently the same. It would certainly have been quicker. Should I do it again from cuttings, I would place a ring of four or five small box plants together to speed it all up, not just one! It was very depressing watching a deflated, balloon-sized ball gradually spread. Ten years on, however, the box balls do give repetition in winter and they help to unite the planting, and so far no box blight! Many ladybirds and other insects find refuge in the box, or around the base.

AVOIDING BOX BLIGHT

My airy garden almost certainly helps to prevent this fungal disease: usually box is more badly affected in walled gardens where the airflow is poor. I am vigilant, though. I keep an eye on it, and when my box is clipped in June, and again in September if needed, great care is taken to rake the bits out of the balls with my fingers. Every snippet is picked up in order to prevent any shoots from rotting down on the ground or inside the bush, and I use a sheet of horticultural fleece as a carpet, making the job easier. I try to clip on a dull day if possible, because

Wallflowers pre-empt the main show

then there's less resin from the leaves to gunge up the clippers and also perhaps less stress on the plant. This tidying up is tedious and time-consuming, taking far longer than the actual snipping, but it seems to be working. Seaweed feed is also applied straight after clipping, because this produces tougher foliage which will hopefully resist box blight should it drift by.

Nearby Cotswold gardens I know have suffered. One local head gardener cut away the infected sections and used seaweed feed, managing to contain the outbreak before it took hold. His large box balls currently have crater-like indentations, but they will recover. In another Cotswold walled garden one section of hedge was cut down to nothing and burnt as soon as the blight was noticed in order to prevent it from spreading to nearby hedges and topiary. The intention was to dig up the infected material, but time restraints meant that it got left in over winter and, the following spring, healthy new growth appeared. The hedge is now as good as new. No fungicides were used in either garden. In Holland, where box blight has been a real problem, the box is cut in winter when spores are less prevalent. This results in fuzzy re-growth in spring, a highly attractive feature, although I'm not sure we'd get it here. Their colder continental climate produces a glorious spring explosion so that tulips and daffodils often share the same stage.

> *One local head gardener cut away the infected sections and used seaweed feed, managing to contain the outbreak before it took hold.*

Taking Box Cuttings

It is an excellent idea to take your own box cuttings from healthy plants. The prime time is August, when the new growth has begun to harden up. The easiest method is to use two plastic flowerpots, one slightly larger than the other. Compost is placed in the bottom of the bigger pot and the cuttings, 7.5–10 cm (3–4 in) in length, are placed round the edge of the pot. The second, smaller, pot is put inside the larger one and the cuttings are kept moist in a cool place (a cold frame is useful here) until spring or autumn, when they are potted up.

Poppy Cat is the least eco-friendly thing in the garden!

LAYOUT

The blocky rectangular shape of the borders mimics the shape of the low-lying cottage. An L-shaped gravel path intersects two main areas and the border furthest away merges into the autumn border with a swathe of blue and lilac phloxes (*Phlox paniculata* 'Franz Schubert' and 'Blue Paradise') set amongst orange and red heleniums (*Helenium* 'Sahin's Early Flowerer' and *H. autumnale* 'Moerheim Beauty') in an attempt to create a seamless flow between the summer border and autumn planting.

The border closest to the house is L-shaped and the planting has a country feel, with scabious, roses, phlox and peonies, all plants that need cold winters to flower well. At the end of the gravel path there's a stone seat made from one of the old porch roofs. The Best Beloved calls this structure 'the mausoleum' because it looks rather stark in winter, but Poppy Cat loves to stretch out on summer evenings when the stone has absorbed that day's heat. Grandchildren also recline, but it wouldn't win any design prizes.

THE BOUNCING BALL

The summer borders on either side of the path contain the same plants, but there is no attempt to create mirror borders with plants directly opposite each other.

Lychnis coronaria 'Gardener's World', not quite out, is bounced along the summer borders

Mirror planting is probably the trickiest planting style of all, because a poor plant or missing plant is very obvious and two plants rarely perform at the same level. It's far easier to bounce the eye along a border by repeat-planting the same thing a little further up so that the eye travels. I used to use a short, dainty oriental poppy called 'Karine' as the bouncing ball, until it succumbed to a mystery disease after a very wet winter. I miss its shallow pink cups blotched in beetroot, for I have not been able to replace it, sadly, and fear that it has gone for ever, for oriental poppies across Europe have been similarly decimated.

I'm now using the double rose campion *Lychnis coronaria* 'Gardeners' World', which has an upright presence, silver woolly foliage and bright-pink to magenta buttons. Being fully double, it cannot set any seeds, as the invasive single forms can. The double form will flower for many months and I have planted an insect-friendly, shorter, pink, single hybrid lychnis called 'Hill Grounds' close by to satisfy the pollinators. This does not set seed, but the single flowers are loved by smaller hoverflies and bees. 'Gardeners' World' is prone to dying out in cold winters, so will probably fade away in time.

CREATE A BACKBONE

All borders need a backbone, a spine of planting that runs through, and floribunda roses do the job here because this area is designed to be at its best in May, June and July. Roses present a unique problem to the organic or natural gardener who cannot and will not spray for black spot (*Diplocarpon rosae*), a fungal disease to which many highly bred roses are prone. The rose loses its black-spotted foliage and lacks vigour as a result, looking miserable. Luckily, there are plenty of roses that do not succumb to black spot disease. Bombproof rose groups include gallicas, rugosas, most ramblers and most species. For a list of bombproof roses, see page 84.

I didn't want to use these in the summer borders at Spring Cottage, though. I wanted repeat-flowering roses that had healthy, glossy foliage

GOLDEN RULE

When planting a border, use a limited selection of plants and plant them in sweeps, not blobs, or in threes, fives or sevens depending on border size. Don't be afraid to repeat a plant along the border.

The soft, champagne-white roses are held in clusters and they appear in July here, slightly later than many roses.

and a shorter stature that would allow me to weave them through *Paeonia lactiflora* hybrids and phloxes, my other two key plants. I stumbled upon a solution by accident when I was given a floribunda rose called 'Champagne Moment' (KORvanaber). Bred by the German rose company Kordes, it had just won the Rose of the Year 2006. I began with one and ended up planting three more because it was so healthy and vigorous. The soft, champagne-white roses are held in clusters and they appear in July here, slightly later than many roses. They look pale in summer sun, but their warm-champagne tones prevent them from looking glacial. White looks harsh here under the summer sky, although I do have some white valerian (*Centranthus ruber* 'Albus') that self-seeds.

The health and vigour of Kordes roses isn't a fluke. This company stopped spraying their rose beds in 1976 because eco-minded young German gardeners had virtually written off the rose as a good garden plant. Initially, whole fields

Rose 'Wildeve' with peonies and valerian

'Pearl Drift' has silver-pink clusters of open flowers

'Olivia Rose Austin' is from David Austin's new breeding programme

of roses went down with disease until fewer than ten healthy specimens were left. They formed the basis of a new breeding programme, and within ten years Kordes had bred a range of healthy, modern roses and German gardeners responded by planting them. They are now grown in many countries and their brave move has inspired other rose breeders to raise healthy roses too, so few trial fields are sprayed nowadays.

All roses have a breeding name in brackets after their commercial name. Those bred by Kordes begin with KOR, but the trade name varies according to the country. In America 'Champagne Moment' is sold under the name 'Lion's Rose', for instance, but the breeding name KORvanaber stays the same across the world. It's always in brackets after the name.

Several David Austin roses have proved healthy for me. I also grow some Harkness roses, because this company is also selecting for disease resistance. Inevitably I have planted some roses that have shown signs of disease; if this happens, they are given another summer because seasons do vary. I have removed two leggy, upright roses that stood proud of the rest of the border: both were Rose of the Year winners, 'Blue Rhapsody' (too leggy here, but a really good blue-tinted rose) and the not-so-good 'Tickled Pink', too upright, not floriferous enough and with hard-to-place orange buds that open to brown-pink flowers. I do use orange roses, though, but always near blue flowers, with coral-tinted peonies.

> *I also grow some Harkness roses, because this company is also selecting for disease resistance.*

I never intended to plant modern floribunda roses because, like many gardeners, I was a bit of a rose snob. However, they are flower-packed, healthy and compact enough to slot into a summer flower border with ease. They avoid being leggy and upright, like the hybrid tea, and they do not have heavy heads like some English roses bred by David Austin. Floribundas have a slightly

'Champagne Moment', a gloriously healthy Kordes rose, is my key rose

'The Lark Ascending', an upright David Austin Rose, is wonderful used with blues

different time clock too, flowering here in July and then flushing again in late September or October.

Pruning is easy. They are cut back slightly in November to prevent wind rock, because floribundas do hang on to lots of foliage in mild winters. The main pruning is done in February, after the worst of the weather is over, and the correct method is to remove the three Ds – the diseased, dying and dead. Look at the shape of the rose and take out any crossing branches or weak shoots so that you form an open goblet shape. Then reduce the length of the main uprights to 45 cm (18 in), making slanting cuts about 1 cm (½ in) above a bud so that the bud stays at the upper end. This allows water to run away from the growing tip.

Pruning in February will produce a flush of new copper-tinted foliage in spring.

Pruning in February will produce a flush of new copper-tinted foliage in spring. I complement this with a trio of tulips that have a perennial tendency. 'Ballerina' (50 cm/20 in), a scented, warm-orange, lily-flowered tulip of great charm, has flowers which echo with the copper-tinted young rose foliage. 'Negrita' (45 cm/18 in), a robust purple, offers a colour contrast. The marbled, pale-purple 'Shirley' (50 cm/20 in) blends with 'Negrita'. These three return year after year for five years or so, although flower size diminishes, as does height. This makes the planting look far more natural than a sweep of uniform tulips resembling guardsmen.

'Negrita' and 'Shirley' are Triumph tulips, originally bred for cut-flower production, so the stems are short and the petals thick. This makes them good in the garden as well as the vase. They perform in the second half of April and last for three weeks or so, so Triumphs should form the basis of any tulip selection. Don't panic if 'Shirley' opens a buttermilk yellow, as I did the first year I grew it. Within a few days purple mottling develops, varying annually according to temperature.

Tulips in the rose and peony border include 'Negrita', 'Shirley', 'Ballerina', 'Barcelona' and 'Rem's Favourite'

Perennial wallflowers, such as *Erysimum* 'Bowles's Mauve' and the black-budded purple and orange 'Parrish's', mix well with tulips, adding more colour in April. They must be sheared back in late spring to reinvigorate them, or they will flower themselves to death. Once the new growth starts, cuttings can be taken too, using the sand-tray method. The seed-raised wands of *Verbascum phoeniceum* 'Violetta' add glints of purple, and the wands are left to self-seed because the grey-green rosettes of this willowy verbascum do not threaten other plants. The pink 'Rosetta' and the white form are not as abundant.

The perennial *Viola cornuta* is an excellent ground-cover plant under roses, creeping up amongst the stems and producing wispy winged flowers from May until July. Cut them back hard to keep them bushy, after their first flourish and then again in early September to promote a mat of new foliage. This tight new growth allows them to overwinter and survive for many a year. Left leggy, they will fade away in hard winters.

THE ICING ON THE CAKE

Peonies are the icing on the Spring Cottage cake and the flowers that I most look forward to because their ample blooms are often highly fragrant. They are a perfect partner for roses. Their foliage is similar in shape and tone and they have the same globular flower shape. *Paeonia lactiflora* hybrids are the most desirable garden peonies (although I do grow species too), because they hang on to their flowers for far longer than the traditional cottage garden peonies of early May (*P. officinalis*), which tend to fade and go in a week or less.

Peonies are a perfect partner for roses.

I must have twenty or more cultivars and most are semi- or double-flowered peonies in shades of pink, pink-red and white. Many have French names straight out of a Parisian telephone directory. Favourites include the lemon-scented white 'Duchesse de Nemours' (Calot, 1856), the silver-pink 'Monsieur Jules Elie' (Crousse, 1888), the lemon-meringue 'Marie Lemoine' (Calot, 1869) and the blush-pink 'Madame Calot' (Biellex, 1856). These French varieties were bred for cut-flower production in the mid-19th century when the nouveau riche were building their grand houses along the wide avenues of Paris. Peony flowers can be picked at the marshmallow stage, when the buds are opening and soft to the touch. They last well in water.

The most popular cut-flower variety even today is the pink 'Sarah Bernhardt' (Lemoine, 1906). However it isn't a great garden peony because it has lax stems. On the plus side it produces lots of smaller flowers. Many peonies are fragrant and most are heavy-headed, so need to be supported by semicircular rusted metal plant supports to stop them swooning. These are the only plants staked at Spring Cottage, which shows how much I value them.

GOLDEN RULE

Double flowers please the gardener, rather than the pollinators. When you use doubles, be sure to surround them with insect-friendly singles and semi-doubles.

Kelways of England began breeding peonies in 1851 at their Somerset nursery, once the largest in the world. Then breeders in North America took up the baton, for the peony is one of the hardiest garden plants of all. In the heartland of the United States, where the continental climate produces a cycle of freezing winters followed by scorching, sun-baked summers, American breeders were far more adventurous about colour. They raised brasher shades, including coral-pink and orange. Like many peony lovers, I was wary about planting anything that wasn't pink, red or white. Then I saw 'Coral Charm'

An unknown scutellaria with bee

thriving in James Fenton's Oxfordshire garden, positioned alongside blue flowers that included amsonia and iris. They were set against a sunset-orange brick wall and my heart skipped a beat, because some young flowers were peachy-orange whilst others had faded to shades of apricot and clotted cream. It was like a Dutch flower painting. I was hooked.

I now grow 'Coral Charm', raised by Samuel Wissing in 1964, a colour break that took twenty years to perfect. I've added 'Coral Sunset' (Wissing and C. G. Klehm, 1981), which can have up to 20 flowers per clump. 'Pink Hawaiian Coral' (R. G. Klehm, 1981) is nearby, but always late into flower. They're positioned close to orange-toned roses such as Harkness's 'Lady Marmalade' (Rose of the Year 2014) and the taller, paler, more-yellow-than-orange David Austin rose 'The Lark Ascending'.

I now grow 'Coral Charm', raised by Samuel Wissing in 1964, a colour break that took twenty years to perfect.

Blue perennials are never far away from these coral peonies. *Geranium* 'Orion', a large, mound-forming hardy geranium with bright-blue saucers, flowers from

May onwards. In late July it's sheared back to the ground and new leaves appear within days. It will re-bloom within four weeks. A skullcap, *Scutellaria*, has dainty spires of blue-and-white flowers and this self-seeds a little in a poor corner of the border where the soil is thin. Further into the border, the substantial purple-pink flowers of *Stachys macrantha* 'Superba' blend with *Geranium* 'Orion', their flowers hardly ever without a bee.

There are also patches of one of the easiest summer bulbs, Triteleia laxa *'Queen Fabiola', and these give a blast of cobalt-blue flower on the southern edge where it's sunniest.*

There are also patches of one of the easiest summer bulbs, *Triteleia laxa* 'Queen Fabiola', and these give a blast of cobalt-blue flower on the southern edge where it's sunniest. They've persisted and bulked up, and the name *laxa* is perhaps misleading, because they slant over the edge of the border rather than flop. My blue-toned penstemons include *Penstemon* 'Stapleford Gem', an erect, substantial penstemon with a faded charm and far paler foliage than most, and *P. heterophyllus*, an early-flowering, prostrate, forget-me-not mixture of pink and blue. I also find room for cupid's dart (*Catananche caerulea*), which produces pointed, papery buds that almost outdo the flowers. It mingles with the floaty grass *Stipa tenuissima*, an 'Evelyn' penstemon and a wiry-stemmed potentilla, *Potentilla nepalensis* 'Ron McBeath'. They sprawl round a box ball on a corner of the border. Blue-stemmed eryngiums, mainly named forms of *Eryngium* × *zabelii*, hold their colour here as well and, when the thimbles are fresh, the buff-tailed bumblebees clamber all over them.

Other glints of blue come from herbaceous clematis, which are so underused in gardens. Dark-blue forms of *Clematis integrifolia* flower from late May and wind themselves up through other plants, such as white astrantia. Pale astrantias, in shades of green, pink and white, arrive in May but need to be cut back before they seed or brown in high-summer sun. Nearer the roses, the classic blue campanula, *Campanula lactiflora* 'Prichard's Variety', is always in flower with the roses. This metre-high form should have deep, violet-blue flowers on a tight head and the beauty is that, if dead-headed, it will flower from lateral buds lower down. It does get woody after three to four years, so taking basal cuttings from the new growth is a good insurance policy. The cool-pink 'Loddon Anna' is close to the house in more shade, and this plant seems to go on year after year. It also responds to dead-heading.

GOLDEN RULE

Extend the season by adding some latecomers to spring, summer and autumn borders.

8 BOMBPROOF ROSES FOR A SUMMER BORDER

'Joie de Vivre' (KORfloci01)
A compact, champagne-tinted, petal-packed Kordes floribunda that was Rose of the Year in 2011, showing more colour than 'Champagne Moment' and with smaller flowers on a lower bush.

'Bonica' (Meidomonac)
This low-growing, pink shrub rose, raised in France by Meilland in 1984, is in the top flight of roses because it's able to thrive and flower on poorer soil. It lines the front path here and is hardly ever out of flower.

'You're Beautiful' (Fryracy)
Bred in England by Gareth Fryer, this Rose of the Year 2013 has large pink flowers that develop a salmon tint as they mature, so this is harder to place than 'Bonica', but worth the effort.

'Olivia Rose Austin' (Ausmixture)
One of David Austin's English roses and the first to be launched from his new breeding programme in 2014. This strongly fragrant, soft-pink rose has flowers with an old-fashioned look set against shiny, mid-green foliage. It repeat-flowers well.

'Pearl Drift' (Leggab)
This low-growing, modern shrub rose, bred by Bill Le Grice in 1980, produces clusters of open, silver-pink flowers over a long period. With parents like 'New Dawn' (a silver-pink, repeat-flowering rambler) and 'Mermaid' (a classic canary-yellow climber with a big boss of stamens), it's not surprising that this rose is so good. It makes a wide shape.

'The Lark Ascending' (Ausursula)
Sunset-yellow shades with an apricot colour wash sum up this David Austin English rose, which has roughly 20 petals arranged in a cup shape. It is upright in habit, very healthy and repeats its lightly fragrant flowers well. It's smooth-stemmed, where many orange-toned roses aren't. Launched in 2012.

'Lady Marmalade' (Hartiger)
This Rose of the Year 2014, bred by Harkness, is very thorny. However, this floribunda produces masses of flowers in a warm, sunset-orange. It has an upright habit, reaching 120 cm (4 ft) here, and is extremely strong and healthy.

'Champagne Moment' (KORvanaber)
A widely available, award-winning Kordes floribunda rose of great strength and vigour. Lots of champagne-white flowers held in large clusters above high-gloss, dark-green foliage. Rose of the Year 2006 among its many awards.

Rose 'Wildeve' with 'Champagne Moment'

Hummingbird hawk-moth on *Centranthus lecoqii*

The colour of 'Loddon Anna' is reflected by a lavender-pink valerian (*Centranthus lecoqii*), which has proved hardy despite coming from Morocco. This mingles with pink valerian and both are highly popular with one prized garden visitor – the hummingbird hawk-moth (*Macroglossum stellatarum*), who does a regular round of the garden, often arriving at four o'clock, which is tea time here. In good summers we can see three or four at once. The Best Beloved has noticed that each hummingbird hawk-moth has a slightly different chequerboard arrangement of white specks on the lower end of its abdomen, making it easy to identify individuals.

One of their food plants, lady's bedstraw, *Galium verum*, grows in the garden in our long grass, forming a vivid yellow haze that signifies summer is here. The hummingbird hawk-moth is a delight to watch, as its hugely long tongue uncoils before your eyes. It's a suspected resident, although most will be immigrants carried to Britain on a warm wind. It will lay eggs on red valerian (*Centranthus ruber*) and it will feed on other plants, although the valerian is top dog. Talking about dogs, the smell of valerian on a damp day is very like wet dog; although unpleasant for the gardener, this is a device to attract flies when the weather is too dull or cool for moths and butterflies to be on the wing. I examined my shoes on the first occasion I noticed the doggy smell, until I realised it was coming from the flowers.

Valerian reproduces fluffy seed-heads, and sadly we can't tell the ordinary pink or white valerian from the lovely soft-lavender *V. lecoqii* at the seedling stage. However, it's such a useful plant, as it's possible to keep valerian in flower from May until October if you dead-head the faded flowers between May and late July. Then, if you shear off the whole thing to stumps in August, this plant will respond and flower again in late autumn. One year we had hummingbird hawk-moths feeding on the last day of October.

> *By July and August the border phloxes have begun to shine and they enjoy the soil in the garden.*

By July and August the border phloxes have begun to shine and they enjoy the soil in the garden. I have many different kinds, but mainly stick to purples, pinks and paler shades. They are very pollinator-friendly, unlike the roses and many of the peonies, and they are scented. Those with drier gardens should grow the pale-pink *P. paniculata* 'Monica Lynden-Bell', the airy white 'Alba Grandiflora', or the variegated pale-pink 'Norah Leigh'. These will even grow on chalk.

Some pink phloxes can be tricky to place because they hover between pink and orange. I like the following: the red-eyed 'Eva Cullum', the pink-eyed 'Bright Eyes' and the all-pink 'Mother of Pearl' and 'Rosa Pastell'. All have the

Phlox paniculata 'Visions'

The papery buds of *Catananche caerulea* with Penstemon 'Evelyn'

AGM, always a reliable indicator of a good plant. All are perfect for a summer herbaceous border, rising to 90 cm (3 ft) or so. Once established, they will perform for many years without needing division, because they're strong, robust varieties. I use purple *P. paniculata* 'Purple Flame', which is a much newer phlox selected from Syngenta Seeds and then raised by cuttings. Purple phloxes do get rain-damaged, although 'Purple Flame' is better than most.

I rate border phloxes because they are self-supporting and both their foliage and their buds are handsome long before the flowers appear. They can suffer from eelworm, stem-borne nematodes that split the stem and distort the leaves. Always cut off any distorted, unhappy-looking stems if you see them, and cut your phlox stems down very low in early autumn, before too many eelworms hibernate in the ground.

Phloxes need space: they find it difficult to push through other plants, so position them carefully.

Phloxes need space: they find it difficult to push through other plants, so position them carefully. They start into growth and emerge early in the year, so most gardeners lift them in September, if dividing or moving, to allow them to settle. They are also shallow-rooted and can get water-stressed. Mildew may strike, but the plants will not suffer in the following year if the summer's damp. They are greedy feeders, but the whole of the summer border is fed in spring with a potash-rich, slow-release feed.

Roses, peonies and phloxes are all rounded and blobby in flower shape, so it's vital to have some vertical accents. One of my most useful is the truly perennial *Verbascum chaixii* 'Album' which performs in July. it produces narrow tapers of damson-blotched white flowers with orange filaments, the latter a feature with all verbascum. It could be used to pick up the orange geum 'Totally Tangerine', or it could tone with purple phloxes or surrey-pruple roses. The small flowers blend into this border and the flowers are adored by Hoverflies. The grey-green arrangement of crinkled foliage is also attractive but, most importantly of all, *V. chaixii* 'Album' is reliably perennial and long-lived. And so many verbascum aren't.

GOLDEN RULE

If you want to grow roses organically, seek out the healthy ones. Prune them well and feed them well.

Hemerocallis provide the sword-like foliage and I have chosen pallid-lemon varieties that are all slightly different. 'Green Flutter', for instance, has full flowers with a puckered texture. I also grow a sterile, bushy evening primrose with pallid flowers held on long stems, probably *Oenothera organensis*. This is propagated from cuttings and will produce flower after flower without the worry of any seeds.

The Japanese anemone 'Pamina' ramps through the summer border a little too enthusiastically

These pale yellows run through this part of the garden like a fine thread and they flatter one of the best August plants ever, the purple and pink *Origanum laevigatum* 'Herrenhausen', the best magnet for small tortoiseshell butterflies.

EXTENDING THE SEASON

The summer border wanes in late July, but gets a new lease of life when the Japanese anemone, *Anemone hupehensis* var. *japonica* 'Pamina', flowers in August. The semi-double pink flowers are held on thick stems and the buds are just like grey seed pearls, so this is a well-loved addition, despite the fact that it rambles through the border. When the plant-hunter Robert Fortune (1812–1880) first saw *A. hupehensis* it was running between the tombstones of a Shanghai graveyard. It's the nature of the beast, and one day I may even regret planting it *en masse* because this is what Japanese anemones do – travel.

Annual cosmos (*Cosmos bipinnatus*) in shades of pink and white come into their own once September arrives, spurred into life by evenly balanced days and nights, conditions they enjoy in their native Mexico. Penstemons also flourish then and both will go on late. *Gaura lindheimeri* will also produce white butterflies softened by pale-pink, and this is often the last summer bloom left standing in the garden, struggling into November. The rhubarb-pink and white flowers begin in July, matching the summer colour palette because there are no brassy yellows or bright oranges. These come later in the autumn border.

TIPS FOR GROWING ROSES ORGANICALLY

- Don't spray your aphids. Instead, allow time for the birds, ladybirds and other predatory insects to discover them. They will lay eggs close by, or predate them directly. Rub out aphids with your fingers if the problem bothers you.

- Use roses in mixed planting rather than in dedicated rose borders, as this lessens the chance of diseases like black spot.

- Underplant your roses with non-invasive herbaceous perennials to prevent fungal spores from splashing up from the bare soil.

- Mulch with well-rotted organic material during winter to create a barrier between soil and rose.

- Feed roses well – once in March and again after the first flush of flowers. Use garden compost, well-rotted manure, or a slow-release or sprinkle-on rose fertiliser.

- Prune roses, making cuts that slope away from the buds and using clean, sharp secateurs. Remove the dead, dying and diseased wood by late spring, keeping the shape open to allow a flow of air.

- Ask specialist rose growers to recommend their healthiest varieties. Prepare the ground well when planting and cut bare-root roses down hard straight after planting to limit wind rock.

- Be bold and replace disease-prone roses with better varieties. Ideally, replace the soil or replant in a slightly different position.

- Use some late-flowering nectar plants to sustain hoverflies and lacewings. Both have predatory larvae which feed on aphids. *Gaura lindheimeri*, annual cosmos and penstemons can sustain insects and bees until late autumn.

Another extremely healthy rose, 'The Generous Gardener' is too large for the summer borders, but I grow it by the summerhouse

Rudbeckia subtomentosa 'Henry Eilers' and *Molinia caerulea*
subsp. *arundinacea* 'Karl Foerster'

CHAPTER 7

AUTUMN INTO WINTER

-7-
AUTUMN INTO WINTER

The autumn border is designed to catch the warmth of the afternoon sun, an important consideration when days are getting shorter and cooler, so it's positioned on the southern to western edges of the garden to soak up all the warmth it can as the year fades. The light shines through, getting lower and lower, right up until the shortest day in December and the vegetation stays intact until late January when everything gets cut down. On dank, deep-winter days the colour palette is an almost military mixture of brown, khaki, grey and black stems and heads. When frost descends, it sparkles. I love this area, whether it's in camouflage fatigues or in glittering ice-queen mode. It offers texture and movement on bleak days when little else stirs.

This border means that late-flying bees and other pollinators can always find some nectar, and I also have some arborescent English ivy (*Hedera helix*) climbing on the back wall, a little way behind the border. This will flower in November, when most things have given up, and it is a really important honeybee plant for this month, which often has a warm patch. Late berries follow. Wrens pick through the autumn border on a daily basis, flitting from stem to stem in search of a ready meal. Robins give it their full attention too, for small insects lurk among the bare stems in cracks and crevices created by the fading grasses and perennials. Spiders and ladybirds lie low now, comforted by the fading foliage just as much as I am. When I cut back in late January the stems are stacked by the compost heap to allow lodging insects an escape route.

Late-season grasses make an impact in this border, and they move and sway, making a huge contribution, particularly during winter when light levels are low. As their panicles disintegrate, their heads create a fine gossamer veil in

> *Late-season grasses move and sway, making a huge contribution, particularly during winter when light levels are low.*

Tall grasses add movement and texture

The banded foliage of *Miscanthus sinensis* 'Zebrinus' with rudbeckia and phlox

winter-white, while low sunlight backlights their form and picks up all the detail. This compensates for the very visible dust on the dresser in my kitchen and the glare through the car's windscreen, the downside of low winter sun.

I rely on several forms of *Miscanthus sinensis*, sometimes called Chinese silver grass, because this provides a mass of good foliage, with airy heads usually held on strong stems above the foliage. 'Zebrinus' is an old cultivar used by Gertrude Jekyll. She knew this green-leafed and golden-banded miscanthus as *Eulalia japonica* and used the foliage to create flecks of light in shady borders. I grow 'Zebrinus' in good light, though, because the golden bands pick up pallid-yellow August daisies such as *Helianthus* 'Lemon Queen'. Although 'Zebrinus' is said to be floppy by some, in my garden it forms a handsome, upright, man-high column with foliage that gracefully curves over at the tips. I much prefer it to the more recent and very vertical 'Strictus'. The common name of this, porcupine grass, says it all.

> *'Zebrinus' is an old cultivar used by Gertrude Jekyll.*

The last grass to flower is *Cortaderia selloana* 'Silver Feather', seen here in early October

Miscanthus flowers frustratingly late at Spring Cottage. If I gardened 70 or so miles further south, or west, the grassy heads would appear in July rather than early September. This difference in flowering times may influence your choice of cultivar, because some, like 'Silberfeder', a 1950s cultivar selected by Hans Simon, are early. In the banana belt of southern England, 'Silberfeder' is often criticised because the flowerheads break up before winter sets in. I, on the other hand, grow 'Silberfeder' because it is *early*. I know I will get flowers by late August or early September. It was also a great favourite of the late Alan Bloom, a pioneer who grew tall grasses in his Dell Garden at Bressingham in Norfolk, and it still has an AGM.

'Graziella' is another early variety to consider. It was raised in Germany by Ernst Pagels (1931–2007) and led to a new race of miscanthus after Pagels persuaded 'Graziella' to set seeds under warm glass in his nursery at Leer during the 1980s. His first batch of seedlings showed great variability, which pleased him, and he deliberately selected those that showed a willingness to flower earlier. He went on to raise some excellent cultivars, including 'Malepartus' and 'Kleine Föntane'. His contribution was invaluable and, when the RHS held their Miscanthus Trial between 1998 and 2003 in which 16 cultivars were awarded the AGM, nine of them had been raised and sent in by Pagels.

Red-tinted miscanthus pick up the colour of mauve and purple asters at first, but their grassy heads soon fade to sable brown.

I'd love to have room for all nine of Pagels' award-winners, but I have to satisfy myself with 'Ferner Östen' – literally Far East – a red-awned miscanthus that flowers very willingly for those of us with chilly gardens. Red-tinted miscanthus pick up the colour of mauve and purple asters at first, but their grassy heads soon fade to sable brown. Despite that they add a richness to the late garden.

I've had less success with a Japanese variegated variety called *M. sinensis* var. *condensatus* 'Cosmopolitan', because cold winters knock this AGM cultivar back so that it has never become truly magnificent for me, despite being planted eight or so years ago. It refuses to form a tight clump and spaces out its stems, perhaps searching for a warm spot. 'Cosmopolitan' is tastefully but brightly variegated, with linear variegation surrounding an all-green inner. It rarely flowers here, so this is definitely a miscanthus grown for foliage; even during the trial at the much warmer RHS Wisley in Surrey, flowers did not appear until November.

Without this flash of wine-red foliage, this whole area, largely dominated by grasses and small-flowered lavender stars, could look anaemic.

As winter beckons, the vertical banding of 'Cosmopolitan' develops hints of pink, picking up the colour of late asters and the purple-red lollipop foliage of *Cotinus coggygria* 'Royal Purple'. This dark-leafed shrub is the touchpaper to several nearby grasses in shades of ivory and cream. It drops its leaves obligingly late, so it's a very useful plant, and the wiry flower heads which give it the name of smoke bush mimic the grassy inflorescences in texture and form. Without this flash of wine-red foliage, this whole area, largely dominated by grasses and small-flowered lavender stars, could look anaemic. In cold autumns cotinus foliage will develop bright-pink margins and flecks – an added bonus.

Ernst Pagels, who bred so many miscanthus, was originally inspired by the German nurseryman Karl Foerster (1874–1970), for whom the young Ernst once worked. Foerster pioneered the use of grasses in natural planting, and in 1940 his catalogue listed 100 different ornamental grasses, plants he described as 'nature's hair'.

I grow two grasses named after Foerster and both are top-notch performers. *Calamagrostis* × *acutiflora* 'Karl Foerster' is a ramrod-straight, feather reed-grass that provides the best vertical accent of all, reaching 1.8 m (6 ft) in height. The young foliage is green and the feathery young heads, which are reminiscent of purple heather on a moor, appear in early summer.

Symphyotrichum 'Little Carlow' is a beacon in any autumn border

Most of my grasses are grown in good, open positions, but the lower-growing Korean feather reed-grass (Calamagrostis brachytricha) *does best in shade.*

At this stage the stems are vulnerable to strong winds and some outer ones may snap. However, this grass, like all the plants I mention, will never need staking. By late summer the whole plant, flowers and foliage alike, will have turned to shades of russet-brown and stiffened to attention, remaining a feature for many months. I have room for only one, but if I could I'd plant a backbone of them.

My other Karl Foerster grass is a tall, airy affair, which turns to golden treacle by autumn. *Molinia caerulea* subsp. *arundinacea* 'Karl Foerster' lies at the front of the border because the foliage is low-growing. The stems are tall and slender, rising to head height, and they provide a golden veil. As the temperatures fall and the light fades, this is like a fine, golden wire sculpture. In October it sets off *Kniphofia rooperi*, a late poker with conical pumpkin-orange heads. It is a wonderful thing to have new flowers in mid-October. It shows that there's still plenty of life in the old dog.

Nearby, another tall, finer-beaded molinia named 'Transparent' lolls around, hanging its heads over the daisies and blue aconitums. I long for showers of rain to cling to the dark beads on these grassy heads. When the sun breaks through, they turn into crystals.

Most of my grasses are grown in good, open positions, but the lower-growing Korean feather reed-grass (*Calamagrostis brachytricha*) does best in shade. It curtsies, flowering in September here, and the silky heads are purple at first. As winter descends, the panicles open, living up to their feathery moniker. It's a quiet grass, tucked away and easily missed, but well worth a place and very good close to the plump, pigeon-breasted *Sedum* 'Matrona'. Both reach around 75 cm (2½ ft).

You couldn't possibly miss two of my grasses. The most dramatic of all is the New Zealand Toe Toe grass (*Cortaderia richardii*), a giant that flowers in July, producing splayed stems topped with cream flowerheads that hang to one side very gracefully.

Kniphofia rooperi with *Molinia caerulea* subsp. *arunolineicea* 'Transparent' in October

The foliage is plain, but slightly silvery, and this grass has an all-year presence. So much so that hedgehogs hibernate in the outer reaches, between the summer house and this grass. Any winter tidying is a cautious, minimalistic exercise because we don't want to disturb a slumbering hedgehog. This is the grass that stops people in their tracks as they walk along the footpath close to the cottage wall. It can be seen, fields away, dwarfing the summer house. The fact that it

> *This is the grass that stops people in their tracks as they walk long the footpath close to the cottage wall.*

flowers in July is a real bonus, because it's lovely for many months of the year. It does need space and will take up a large slice of a border, probably 4 sq. m (4½ sq. yards), and rises to 4 m (13 ft).

My other cortaderia is a much shorter, variegated pampas grass called *C. selloana* 'Silver Feather' (Norcort), which reaches only 1.2 m (4 ft) or so. This variegated sport from *C. selloana* 'Pumila' was nurtured and hand-propagated by Notcutts' propagation manager Ivan Dickings before being launched in 1998. It pops out its flowers in early October and is one of the latest things to flower, so highly appreciated for that reason. I love to see the silky buttermilk tassels unfurl from a cigarillo of finely variegated leaf, showing at first a tassel and then, finally, a plume the size of a giant corn on the cob.

'Silver Feather' produces at least 70 stems that splay outwards, held above fine foliage, so in winter it's glorious in foliage and flower. The heads are removed in March, or earlier if they are breaking up, and the foliage may also be tidied with the aid of stout gloves. All pampas grass foliage will cut and wound, and that may dictate its position in your garden, or whether you grow it or not. The stems must be shredded and chopped, such is the resilience of this graceful grass, because it never rots down on the heap.

GOLDEN RULE

Leave some late-flowering flowers intact over winter to shelter insects and birds, etc. Most are stiff-stemmed enough to provide winter silhouettes, but you may wish to remove some troublesome seed-heads.

'Silver Feather' is one of my favourites, and yet pampas grass has a bad press. It's associated with suburban planting, and you see them plonked into lawns in front of bungalows, looking shabby. It was a great Victorian favourite, championed and planted by William Robinson (1838–1935) of Gravetye Manor in West Sussex. He first saw it growing at the Glasnevin Botanic Garden in Dublin while visiting. Glasnevin

Eupatorium maculatum 'Atropurpureum' is a fantastic partner for *Helianthus* 'Yellow Queen'

had introduced the grass in 1840 and Robinson, who summed it up as 'noble, distinct and beautiful', used it at his next post at Regent's Park in London. After that it became wildly popular. He referred to it rather lovingly in his book *The Wild Garden: Or Our Groves and Shrubberies Made Beautiful by the Naturalisation of Hardy Exotic Plants*. Quite!

Tall grasses need tall perennials if the border is going to flow. Luckily, most taller plants have a tendency to flower in autumn because it takes them a lot of time to reach their full height. Many of them are daisies, with hundreds of tiny flowers clustered in button middles beset by a ruff of colourful ray petals. Butterflies land on them easily. Hoverflies adore the colour of the yellow middles, as do bees, and the flowers are long-lasting.

Rudbeckia fulgida var. deamii
starts in August

Succisa pratensis 'Peddar's Pink'
is a bumblebee favourite

Yellow daisies are especially attractive to bees and hoverflies, and their flowers
run through the border like a golden thread, clashing against blue, bright-pink
and purple, and blending harmoniously with orange and warm-red. The yellows
can come in confident warm shades or cooler pallid-yellow, so generally they
look best buffered by stronger colours. *Helianthus*
'Lemon Queen', a star plant, is a mass of small,
cool-lemon flowers held at eye height and in a warm
season it can astound you with its generosity. It
makes a robust clump and may need culling every
fourth or fifth year, but little can rival this tall
daisy for flower power. Position it carefully, or you
may only see the backs of the flowers, because they
track the sun as many helianthus or sunflowers do. On the plus side, it will
still be flowering in October. 'Lemon Queen' was raised by Thomas Carlile of
the Loddon Nurseries in Twyford near Reading in Berkshire *circa* 1930. He

> *Yellow daisies are especially
> attractive to bees and hoverflies,
> and their flowers run through the
> border like a golden thread.*

Aster amellus 'King George'.
The best form of the Italian aster

Vernonia crinita is a tall
purple aster-like plant

considered it too special to be given his usual prefix of Loddon, but if you see that name on any yellow daisy, buy it. Loddon varieties are all excellent.

'Lemon Queen' is the perfect partner for equally tall wine-red eupatoriums. These produce cloud-like puffs of flower despite being in the daisy family. The one I love most is the black-stemmed *Eupatorium maculatum* 'Riesenschirm' (meaning 'Gigantic Umbrella' in German), with its whorls of green leaf topped by storm clouds that never seem without a butterfly or two. I'm not warm enough here to be troubled by unwanted seedlings, which can be a problem in hotter places. Both 'Lemon Queen' and 'Riesenschirm' need a warm summer to perform well and both do best on good soil. Spring drought reduces the stature of both, but if all goes well both will attain 1.5 m (5 ft) or more. The mixture of lemon and wine, served up just as summer gives way to autumn, is as irresistible to the gardener as it is to the pollinator. Slugs can damage the asparagus-like spears of the eupatorium as they

> *'Lemon Queen' is the perfect partner for equally tall wine-red eupatoriums.*

Grasses persist through winter adding form and movement

push through the ground and the spears are quite late to emerge, so do label their position so that you don't trample them to death.

Nearby is the best umbellifer ever, *Selinum wallichianum*, which produces white flower heads, similar to those of the eupatorium, along with lacy green foliage held by bloomed purple stems and sheaths. Pink echinaceas pick these up very well.

The best yellow daisy for a long run of flower is *Rudbeckia fulgida* var. *deamii* because it produces a neat rounded bush, about 90–120 cm (3–4 ft) in height, with masses of clean, golden-yellow flowers with tight brown middles. The similar seed-raised 'Goldsturm' is not quite as neat, with larger, brasher yellow flowers produced

The best yellow daisy for a long run of flower is **Rudbeckia fulgida** *var.* **deamii** *because it produces a neat rounded bush with masses of clean, golden-yellow flowers.*

If you've struggled with heleniums before, 'Sahin's Early Flowerer' is a stronger hybrid that repeat-flowers

An August explosion of *Kniphofia* 'Prince Igor'

Crocosmia 'Lucifer' begins in July

a little later. The European hybrid aster, *Aster × frikartii* 'Mönch', makes an excellent partner for shorter yellow rudbeckias if you don't mind two daisies rubbing shoulders together. This drought-tolerant aster flowers for longer than any other and the long-lashed, lavender-blue daisies begin in July, before many others. The dark-green foliage does not detract from the flowers at any stage and the slightly lax habit allows it to slot into the border well. Hybrid vigour allows 'Mönch' to survive without division, but, like all autumn-flowering plants, if you do need to divide do so in spring – just as the growth gets going. Autumn divisions of most spring-flowering plants generally perish.

The willowy *Rudbeckia laciniata* 'Herbstsonne', literally meaning 'Autumn Sun', is another star performer. It's long-lived and easily grown. Each flower has drooping outer yellow petals surrounding a green cone that gradually turns darker as the bees work their magic. The common name of coneflower reflects the inner thimble's shape. It's 2.2 m (7 ft) at least, but stands here without being staked, generally losing its petals by early October. Snails do find the lobed foliage tasty in spring and early summer, so be wary.

At the other end of the height chart is the crisp *R. triloba*, a small, dark-eyed yellow daisy that shines in September and October. Some report seedlings, but there have never been any here, which is a shame, for this rudbeckia has a tendency to be short-lived. Despite its death wish, *R. triloba* is a mass of neat, inch-wide flowers in rich brown and sunny yellow. I often grow some annual *R. hirta* too, and prefer the large, flat-topped yellow daisies of 'Indian Summer' to the others. In mild winters these will come through, indicating that they are slightly tender perennials rather than annuals. Both will reach 90 cm (3 ft) or so.

> *Despite its death wish,* **R. triloba** *is a mass of neat, inch-wide flowers in rich brown and sunny yellow.*

The heleniums in this border add shades of brown, orange and red. The most successful is 'Sahin's Early Flowerer', a hybrid that tolerates drier soil and begins in July. Each flower is different, so this plant dazzles in a border, and this helenium will re-bloom, so it's worth dead-heading it meticulously. The brown

Hesperantha 'Pink Princess'

velvet middles attract hordes of bees, and leafcutter bees, with their pollen-covered undersides, seem to match the flowers. 'Sahin's Early Flowerer' reaches 1.2 m (4 ft) or so and it's grown with blue and lavender phloxes that include *P. paniculata* 'Blue Paradise' and 'Franz Schubert'. I also grow the tall, much-later *Helenium autumnale* 'Flammenspiel' and this reaches over 1.5 m (5 ft) in height here. The translation 'Dancing Flame' suits this red-orange helenium very well.

There are flashes of orange-red throughout this border and it's a touchpaper colour for blues – whether it's *Symphyotrichum* 'Little Carlow', *Aconitum carmichaelii* 'Arendsii' or *A.* 'Spark's Variety' – all plants grown here. The most vivid orange plant of all

> *The most vivid orange plant of all is a mighty August-flowering kniphofia named 'Prince Igor'.*

is a mighty August-flowering kniphofia named 'Prince Igor'. This produces 30–40 spikes of orange flowers, or more, and these are adored by wasps, who flock here in search of a sugar fix. Brush up against the flowers and they will shower you with droplets of sugar-sweet nectar, and I have seen sparrows drinking once or twice! In the wild it would be sunbirds.

There are crocosmias too, beginning with the tomato-red 'Lucifer' in July. This almost edible-looking crocosmia provides bright, branching, Bloody Mary flowers and sword-shaped, bright-green leaves that add definition to the border, providing vertical accents long after the flowers have gone. Later-flowering crocosmias include the all-yellow, front-of-border 'Columbus', the

> *This almost edible-looking crocosmia provides bright, branching, Bloody Mary flowers.*

salmon-pink 'Okavango' and the completely red 'Hellfire', among others. Red has a magical quality: it fixes all the other colours in the spectrum and should be part of any border if you can manage it. Just a touch will do the job.

More upright presence is gained from tall, bobble-headed sanguisorbas in shades of maroon and pink. 'Blacksmith's Burgundy', roughly 1.5 m (5 ft) in height, has dark, rounded bobbles that turn almost black later in the year. 'Blackthorn' is shorter, with pink bottlebrushes. 'Cangshan Cranberry' is late and produces long, dark-maroon, caterpillar-shaped bobbles held vertically. I also have a soft-pink, fluffy form of *Sanguisorba hakusanensis*, although this flowers from August onwards. The bobbly ones have a proteinaceous scent that attracts flies, but those with fluffier flowers are sweetly scented and adored by butterflies and bees. Taller sanguisorbas marry well with tall grasses and their winter silhouettes are charming, although self-seeding can be a problem.

Pink, lavender-blue and purple asters play a large part in this border, and the fact that most don't flower until September never bothers me, for their foliage and emerging buds are almost as good as flowers. *Symphyotrichum* (one of the new names for some of the American asters) feature, and they include two New England asters, *S. novae-angliae* 'Helen Picton', a strong purple, and 'Andenken an Alma Pötschke', a raspberry-pink. These September-flowering asters, loved by butterflies, are strong-stemmed and easy to grow. They survive from year to year without regular division, unlike the fussier *S. novi-belgii* ones, which fade away when left to their own devices. The only fault with New England asters is a

> *The only fault with New England asters is a tendency to produce ragged foliage underneath the flowers, but this is remedied by clever positioning within the border.*

tendency to produce ragged foliage underneath the flowers, but this is remedied by clever positioning within the border. Several autumn border flowers need this treatment, including *Thalictrum lucidum*, a lime-green puff of floral smoke, and some monardas. They go in the depths of the border rather than the front, so any browning foliage or ugly legs stay hidden.

Colchicum 'Nancy Lindsay' is the first of many

Later asters include a small-flowered branching variety that I bought as 'Vasterival'. It has dark, wiry stems and branching heads of pink-lavender flowers held in sprays at a height of 1.2 m (4 ft) or so. It originally came from the French village of Vasterival where there are two famous gardens. One is the late Princess Sturdza's garden and the other a Jekyll and Lutyens garden named Le Parc de Moutiers. This aster was found in the latter and is now being sold under two names, 'Les Moutiers' and 'Vasterival'. They are the same, however, and this feminine aster, adored by flower arrangers, tumbles through the border like waves of the sea on a slightly dull day. Vasterival itself is close to the sea in Normandy, so perhaps that's why.

> *This feminine aster, adored by flower arrangers, tumbles through the border like waves of the sea on a slightly dull day.*

Further back, the dark sturdy stems of *Symphyotrichum laeve* 'Calliope' produce lilac-blue daisies set off by almost black foliage and stems. Dark glints of foliage are always welcome, and this aster is another easy perennial that returns year after year. Another form, this time with lilac-pink flowers, is 'Glow in the Dark'. I also grow *Heliopsis helianthoides* var. *scabra* 'Summer Nights', a dark-stemmed, July-flowering heliopsis with branching stems that support small, upward-facing yellow daisies, each with a warm hint of red in their middles. It struggles up in the midst of the border in July, announcing that this area is about to come to life.

My latest aster often waits until mid-October here before it produces tiny blue flowers on an umbrella of smoky stems. It's now named *Symphyotrichum turbinellum* (previously *Aster turbinellus*) but if my garden was warmer it would flower in August. It provides a haze of blue stars, their small size compensated by their sheer numbers. The dusky foliage clings round the purple stems, and it's rather like having a puff of smoke rising up from green wood.

There are also new flowers in late autumn, and I welcome the pale saucers of *Hesperantha* 'Pink Princess' (syn. 'Wilfred H. Bryant'). Previously *Schizostylis*, these go so well with the swooning colchicums such as 'Nancy Lindsay' and 'Dick Trotter'. A few sternbergia, yellow crocus-like flowers, may also show now. Closer to the house there are nerines in shades of pink, catching the falling beech leaves as two seasons collide. *Cyclamen hederifolium* also appears, its large corms bearing masses of jaunty flowers in pink, magenta and white, then as winter marches through the door the foliage, which comes in silver and frosted greens, takes over.

By the time November arrives I know that there will be only two fallow months here.

It all means that the garden still skips along, even though the temperatures are plummeting almost as fast as the days are shortening. By the time November arrives I know that there will be only two fallow months here, and even those will be punctuated by the first autumn-flowering snowdrops and the flowers of *Viburnum* × *bodnantense* 'Dawn', which will appear in clement interludes.

Yellow rattle (*Rhinanthus minor*) just beginning to set seed

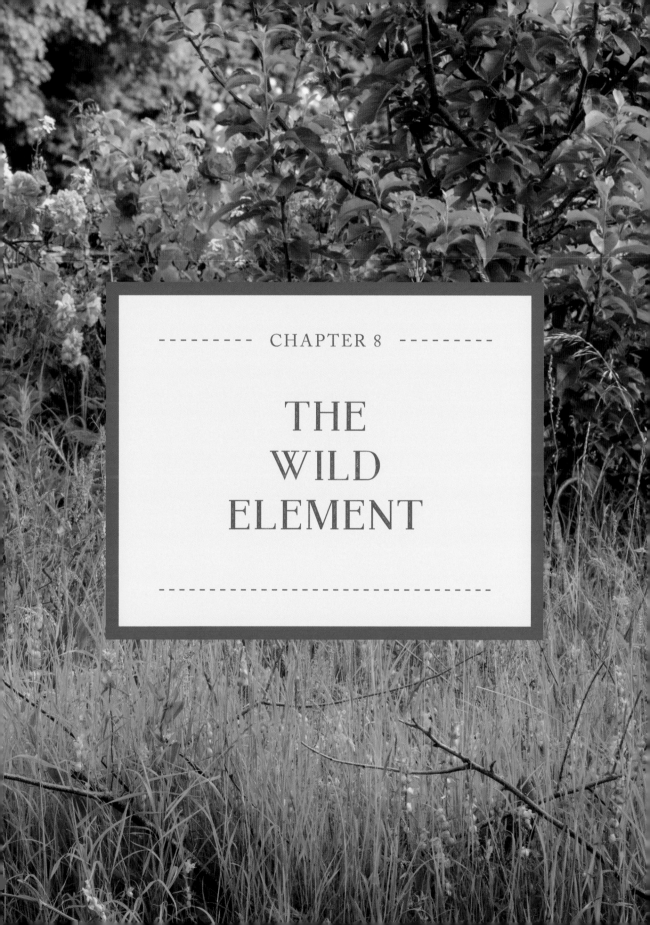

THE
WILD
ELEMENT

-8-
THE WILD ELEMENT

It's very tempting to liken gardening to cleaning the house or the car and spruce it up so that every inch is pristine and manicured. Modern tools such as the strimmer and leaf vac make it far easier than it's ever been and encourage many to go down the tidy route. Indeed, I once listened to an eminent gardener explain that the frogs got in the way of his strimming in long grass and he was always chopping their legs off! The suggestion that these helpful creatures were worth their place in his garden seemed to fall on deaf ears. I do wonder if he's still doing it. Hopefully not!

This type of spick-and-span gardening is a 'no-no' if you want a self-sustaining, eco-friendly garden, but I'm not suggesting you let the entire garden go wild. Parts of my garden are highly manicured, especially those closest to the house, but I also have undisturbed areas and some long grass so that creatures such as frogs have some shelter and refuge. The trick is to make sure that the long grass looks as though it should be there, and the main mini-meadow at Spring Cottage has an antler-like arrangement of sticks as an edging. The antler sticks are removed every September and then replaced in early spring with new ones, just as the grass begins to grow. The mower mows right up to the edge of the sticks, so that there's a sharp definition between the neat lawn and the meadow. This clean line makes it look gardened and the resulting mini-meadow mirrors the fields beyond the wall, extending the garden and borrowing the landscape.

I have to confess that I used to be much tidier than I am now. However, I had a complete change of heart about twenty years ago. I was collecting leaves under a hedge on the north side of my old house, Homefield in Hook Norton. It was November and the beech leaves were damp, cold and claggy, so I put on some very thick gloves and began to fill the wheelbarrow. I had the telephone outside and it rang. I had to take my gloves off to answer it.

The antler-like arrangement of sticks
around the main meadow

Looking from the neat lawn, through the mini-meadow to the undisturbed area by the wall

When I came back after the call I couldn't find my gloves anywhere. I'm sure there's a glove goblin in everyone's garden. The light was fading, so I decided to carry on with my bare hands and almost immediately felt a largish lump in the leaves. It was a hibernating toad, so I ran my hands through the leaf-litter already in the barrow and there were several toad lumps, newt lumps and a frog lump. I ought to explain that I had two ponds at that time in my old garden and this sheltered spot, in the rain shadow of the house, was obviously a preferred hibernation site. I spent the next hour carefully replacing the leaves under the hedge. In this case the glove goblin did me a favour.

> *I decided to carry on with my bare hands and almost immediately felt a largish lump in the leaves. It was a hibernating toad.*

As a result of this hands-on experience, I began to leave leaf-litter alone far more and I quickly noticed that some leaves can look wonderful on the ground. Hazel leaves make a very dry, russet-brown litter, and wood anemones and hellebores love to push up through it as wildflowers do in the wild. *Viburnum* × *bodnantense* 'Dawn' sheds almost grey-black leaves, which also curl and dry, framing foliage

The hedgehog day roost, right by the wall, is clearly visible in winter and early spring

plants attractively. I referred to this leafy layer as the insect duvet in *The Natural Gardener*, and if you pick up a handful of leaves there's often a tiny spider or an unknown bug or two. So leave your leaves to lie where you sensibly can.

Spring Cottage gets covered in beech leaves and these fall late, in batches, and lie very wet, so they are picked up in the borders and on the lawn because they take an age to rot down *in situ*. In wet, mild winters every leaf seems to come with its own baby slug, so I collect the beech leaves from key areas and make leaf mould, using the type of square sacks in which builders deliver sand, etc. I wear thin gloves when doing this and keep my eyes open. I always find some ladybirds roosting, normally 7-spots, and the large square bags of leaves are left open to the elements to allow any creatures like these to escape

> *Spring Cottage gets covered in beech leaves and these fall late, in batches, and lie very wet.*

when they're ready. It takes me two years to get good leaf mould, because it's not turned, and the crumbly friable material is used to top-dress the trillium area in my woodland garden. I would love to make enough for the whole garden, but don't have enough leaves.

I do enjoy leaf gathering – an hour or so here and there in early winter never goes amiss. It might be partly influenced by the American poet Robert Frost (1874–1963), who wrote in his poem 'Gathering Leaves':

I make a great noise
Of rustling all day
Like rabbit and deer
Running away.

The low stone walls that surround Spring Cottage have lots of nooks and crannies for rodents, bees and insects, so I have as many wild areas in their lee as possible. I often feel embarrassed about this, because some people make a special journey to see my garden from the outside looking in. If they peer over the western wall, the strip is deliberately unkempt and they may think the whole garden's the same. An area that abuts the southern wall is also left untended, with a tangle of forgiving shrub roses, including hybrid musks such as 'Wilhelm' and 'Buff Beauty', struggling with forms of our native woodbine, such as *Lonicera periclymenum* 'Graham Thomas' and 'Serotina'. In high summer this looks wonderful from both sides of the wall.

There are some garden plants in this area for spring interest. *Epimedium* × *versicolor* 'Sulphureum' and *Polygonatum* × *hybridum* 'Betberg', a form of Solomon's seal with chocolate stems in spring, are rugged enough to do well there. There are cowslips, including bee-friendly singles and un-bee-friendly doubles, plus some hellebores and ferns also for spring interest. In summer the hardheads (*Centaurea nigra*) appears, to the delight of bumblebees. Purple-pink cornflowers held in diamond-patterned buds are left to self-seed. Soapwort (*Saponaria officinalis*) also thrives here.

> *I know this area is rich in wildlife because Poppy Cat sits for hours poised to pounce.*

Weeds creep in under the walls in this area, so by late summer I am plucking out the bindweed, reaching in rather than treading, though. I know this area is rich in wildlife because Poppy Cat sits for hours poised to pounce. This is prime territory for her, and when the grass and herbage is cut back here in September there are vole nests lined with moss and feathers. The area is clipped by hand, very sedately, because so much lurks within. Ground beetles curl up at the base of the grassy tussocks and by then they crawl rather than scurry away, due to lower temperatures.

We always find the hedgehog's summer roost now, a moss-lined bed constructed like an Anderson shelter. We often hear noise at roughly midday, although that may be because we're out there snatching a sandwich. Grunts that could come from a small pig and thudding noises of great volume can be heard in late spring, but on furtive investigation it seems to be a single hedgehog rather than the two we

> *We always find the hedgehog's summer roost now, a moss-lined bed constructed like a mossy Anderson shelter.*

imagined. I'm sure it is the peace in that area that ensures that on most days we can see the calling card of a hedgehog. (For more on hedgehogs, see Chapter 10.) This wilder area also has some dead wood, an old tree trunk placed *in situ*,

Roses and honeysuckle (*Lonicera periclymenum*) 'Graham Thomas' and 'Belgica' spilling over the wall in this undisturbed area

In spring the main meadow contains fritillarias, cowslips and pasque flowers

to encourage wood-boring beetles, and there's a beehive composter that voles seem to use as a hotel. It's a Sleeping Beauty area, deliberately left to nature, but bordered by a neatly cut path.

In other areas close to the wall there are narcissi and snowdrops for spring flower, interspaced with hardy geraniums, such as the magenta-pink 'Patricia', the deep-blue 'Orion' and the sky-blue 'Rozanne'. Vincas, pulmonarias and ferns are also planted along the walls, together with colchicums, and all these plants are accompanied by roses, including the hybrid musk 'Felicia', 'The Generous Gardener', 'Princess Anne' and 'England's Rose' among others. They are all shades of pink. 'The Generous Gardener', a large rose needing space, is a soft silver-pink. 'Princess Anne' is a strong, blue-pink, upright rose, and 'England's Rose' is a similar colour, described as cherry-pink. These last three, bred by David Austin, have proved healthy and vigorous.

My neighbours have two donkeys, Martha and Dylan, who are adept at pruning roses and are especially fond of the buds.

My neighbours have two donkeys, Martha and Dylan, who are adept at pruning roses and are especially fond of the buds.

THE SPRING BULB LAWN

There are two grassy areas at Spring Cottage. One, near the house, is a spring bulb lawn, because there were old varieties of daffodil in this garden popping up everywhere. We tried to conserve them and either planted them here or

Pasque flowers (*Pulsatilla vulgaris*) thrive in the sunnier spots of the mini-meadow

put them on the wilder edges close to the walls. These simple narcissi flower in March and there are also Dutch crocus, principally the silver-grey and mauve 'Vanguard' and the purple and white stripy 'Pickwick'. Other bulbs include *Ornithogalum nutans*, the drooping star of Bethlehem, with its grey-and-white flowers in April. *Scilla litardierei*, the amethyst meadow squill, is also April-flowering, with tight conical heads of soft-blue stars. These have both naturalised and hopefully will spread further through the grass. In early June this bulb lawn is mowed six weeks or so after the bulbs have flowered and then kept mown for the rest of the year.

THE MAIN MEADOW

The main mini-meadow, in the heart of the garden, follows a different regime. It begins with bulbs that include crocus, narcissi and two fritillarias – *Fritillaria pontica* and *F. pyrenaica*, both of which are robust enough to thrive in grass and set seeds. *F. pontica* has slender green bells edged in brown-maroon, while *F. pyrenaica* has wider bells that tend to be browner. Both come back year after year, each time spread a little further via their seeds. They choose their own spots. There are some camassias too and some pasque flowers, *Anemone pulsatilla*. So in spring it's a colourful mix.

By early June this annual is flowering, producing sunshine-yellow flowers that resemble beaky birds peeping out from a green leafy cup.

When the bulbs are flowering it's possible to see the seedlings of yellow rattle, *Rhinanthus minor*, appearing like green jagged snowflakes on the ground. By early June this annual is flowering, producing sunshine-yellow flowers that resemble beaky birds peeping out from a green leafy cup. Being annual, it must be left to self-seed, and when the seed-heads are ripe they make a noise in the wind, hence the name yellow rattle. This is the meadow staple, because yellow rattle is hemi-parasitic and it feeds on the roots of grasses, subduing coarser grasses. This thins the sward, allowing the seedlings to get a hold in the bare earth, and it creates space for other plants to appear in the gaps too.

I established yellow rattle with ease by shearing off the grass in September about nine years ago using an old Flymo lawnmower. This left virtually no grass, like a

No. 1 haircut on a small boy. I distressed the bare earth with a metal-tined lawn rake, scratched it about and then sprinkled yellow-rattle seed, obtained from a nearby friend's meadow, straight on to the ground and trod it in with a soft-shoe shuffle. It grew, because annual plants have a genuine need to germinate. Seeds can be acquired from seed companies specialising in wildflowers. Luckily, my yellow rattle has reappeared every year in great abundance and it attracts a black bee that doesn't seem to go to other plants.

We also have an acid-yellow froth from lady's bedstraw (Galium verum), *which is a plant of impoverished soil.*

Some meadow grasses have returned, including crested dog's-tail (*Cynosurus cristatus*), characterised by grassy heads that are flat on one side, revealing a herringbone pattern. Known to be a lowland species, it must have thrived here in the past at 200 m (700 ft) above sea level. Sweet vernal-grass (*Anthoxanthum odoratum*), very stiff-stemmed and aromatic, is also present, forming tight, cylindrical heads. Wildflowers, popping up on their own, include hop trefoil (*Trifolium campestre*), a legume with creamy, spherical heads held above the ground. We also have an acid-yellow froth from lady's bedstraw (*Galium verum*), which is a plant of impoverished soil. Meadow vetch (*Vicia cracca*) is also present, as is the yellow-flowered bird's-foot trefoil (*Lotus corniculatus*). Recently *Lathyrus pratensis* appeared and we have a small sedge which self-seeds, *Carex spicata*. I'm happy to allow wildflowers free rein, for the one thing I have learned is that a meadow is dynamic. It changes from year to year. Things disappear, then come back of their own accord.

I'm happy to allow wildflowers free rein, for the one thing I have learned is that a meadow is dynamic.

The one plant that hasn't returned yet, of its own accord, is the hardy orchid, so I've resorted to planting commercially grown hybrid hardy orchids (*Dactylorhiza fuchsii* and its hybrids) in the grass in the hopes of reintroducing the right mycorrhizal fungi to encourage any wild seed in the soil's seed bank to germinate. Orchids set huge amounts of fine seeds, and the late Christopher Lloyd used to transfer his top seedlings to his garden borders because they bulked up faster and then were amenable to division. This goes against the modern myth that all orchids need impoverished soil. I am hoping to get seedlings too, but Christopher Lloyd had a head start. His mother, Daisy, began planting the orchids at Great Dixter over a hundred years ago.

I find hardy orchids beguiling in summer, with their 'stand-to-attention' military presence and lipped flowers, mottled and splashed. The bees find them

I have planted nursery-grown hardy orchids

Yellow rattle is adored by bees

attractive too, lured by scent and the spotting which guides them in. Orchids do not offer nectar, but as a bee searches for it, the orchid's sticky pollen sacs adhere to the bee's head and any pollen sacs that have been deposited cannot be removed by grooming. When the bee visits another flower, though, some of the pollen is transferred, because the flower's stigmatic fluid is even stickier. The process is repeated and copious amounts of fine, dust-like seeds are formed.

No grass cutting takes place until the orchids set seed, so it can be as late as mid-September in this area.

No grass cutting takes place until the orchids set seed, so it can be as late as mid-September in this area. The edging sticks are removed and the sward, which is hand cut because it's a relatively small area, is allowed to lie for a day or two before being collected. Theoretically this will allow more seed-heads to dehisce (split open) as the herbage lies flat on the ground. Then the material is collected and transferred to the compost heap, because if it were allowed to lie and rot down it would add a lot of extra nitrogen and promote the coarser grasses at the expense of wildflowers.

These areas of long grass attract a huge number of insects because so many of our native pollinators have a unique relationship with a certain type – or even one single species – of wildflower. The area also moves and sways, like the field beyond the garden wall, and the grasses and native flowers attract more butterflies than when we first moved here, as they come to roost and lay eggs on their food plants. I have had to restrict red sorrel (*Rumex acetosella*) because it self-seeds relentlessly throughout the garden, and in any case there is plenty in the field beyond, so much so that it can have a rhubarb-pink glow in high summer. Red sorrel is the food plant for the small copper (*Lycaena phlaeas*) and we have these in numbers within

Our longer grass and meadow flowers have increased the number of ringlets

A male gatekeeper feeding on *Origanum laevigatum* 'Herrenhausen'

the garden. They often flock to thymes and marjoram, and recently we had five on the same small plant of *Origanum vulgare* 'Compactum'.

Our increased numbers of butterflies are almost certainly owing to this area of long grass providing the shelter and food plants for them. Our findings match those of the National Trust, which ten or so years ago restricted mowing on financial grounds because it took up too many man hours and used precious fossil fuels. Within two years the Trust's butterfly expert, Matthew Oates, had noticed greater numbers of butterflies, particularly the Browns. This family, whose caterpillars feed on grass species, includes ringlets, graylings, gatekeepers, meadow browns, speckled woods and marbled whites. We also see more skippers. The females lay their eggs haphazardly, scattering them on suitable grasses, and the eggs overwinter low on the ground.

There's evidence (from Butterfly Conservation) that wet summers can be beneficial for grassland butterflies, because the thicker sward offers more protection. The incessant rain during the summer of 2012 'prompted substantial grass growth and

GOLDEN RULE

Leave some areas undisturbed in the outer edges of your garden and cultivate some long grass into a mini-meadow. Cut these areas after the plants have self-seeded and collect all the clippings before they decompose and dump lots of nitrogen.

The meadow brown has only
one eyespot

A marbled white butterfly on knapweed
(*Centaurea scabiosa*)

provided good conditions for some grassland species such as the Meadow Brown, Ringlet and Gatekeeper.' The Wider Countryside Butterfly Survey (WCBS) revealed that the meadow brown enjoyed its best year since the start of the scheme, with almost twice as many counted as in 2011.

I wouldn't be without this mini-meadow because it has enriched my garden in so many ways. Mostly it's easily managed, although the clipping by hand is time-consuming. We have some ancient ant hills in it and the green woodpecker appears in summer to probe them, usually on damp, warm days. It's quite a sight (see page 185).

THE ROADSIDE VERGES

The verges offer more scope, and I can see more species of wildflowers within my garden and on my verge than I can anywhere else in my village, because everybody else mows throughout the season. The Best Beloved, a scientist through and through, has taken to counting the flowers and there are thousands, many of them tiny, at any one time. Crosswort (*Cruciata laevipes*) was particularly testing to count (20 tiny flowers per whorl, half a dozen whorls per stem), but the Best Beloved estimated we had 20,000 crosswort flowers in all, as well as 375 cowslip flowers (8 flowers per stem). Being tiny flowers, they attract

Our verges, which are cut once in early September, begin with cowslips

tiny insects. In June we estimated that there were 900 flowers per square metre of verge. Mown verges close by had only three flowers or fewer per square metre.

Verges are contentious things. Many people see the shorn-grass look as being neat and tidy. However, the charity Plantlife pointed out that more than 700 species of wild plants – almost half the native flora of the British Isles – are found on roadside verges. One in ten of these plants is at risk of extinction, in part because councils cut verges too early, before the plants have set seed.

97 per cent of meadows have been destroyed in England since the 1930s due to the use of herbicides and fertilisers.

Tiny mini-meadows and flower-rich verges would not be so important if we still had flower-filled meadows in the countryside. However, 97 per cent of meadows have been destroyed in England since the 1930s through the use of herbicides, fertilisers and agricultural improvement. The fields beyond my house have never been ploughed, yet they are flower-poor affairs because broad-leafed herbicides have been applied in the past, as well as artificial fertilisers. It all means that the roadside verge is becoming an important natural habitat for wildlife such as bees and other insects.

Plantlife, an excellent charity to belong to, started a petition in 2015 asking local authorities to allow plants on verges to complete their full lifecycle – to grow, flower and set seed. They have also asked for the removal of grass cuttings to lessen the nitrogen released, because this decomposition process increases soil fertility and encourages coarse grasses and weeds such as cow parsley. Plantlife is confident that wildflowers can return if verge management allows it.

Verges have improved locally in this area and can be glorious in some years. However, it only takes a tractor and gang mower, used at the wrong time in the wrong place, to decimate next year's display, as I know in my own parish. Our protected verge was cut early by mistake two years running, despite being listed for late cutting only. It went backwards, undoing ten years of hard work.

THE MAIN PIECES IN YOUR LIVING JIGSAW

I believe that the most useful thing gardeners can do, when it comes to managing their plot, is to have a wild element within their garden, containing longer grass and some wildflowers. You can make it look attractive by manicuring the areas nearby, and it may be more important than you think.

I couldn't possibly cover every living thing in my garden, but I've picked out the main players and segregated them into the three chapters that follow – 'The Dreaded Gastropod', 'The Flying Squad' and 'The Ground Force'. I make no attempt to separate sinners and saints, because the whole concept of this book is to see the living jigsaw as a series of interactions or food chains. Despite my best attempts, the very fact that I have given slugs and snails their own section has led to some overlapping, but that's the nature of ecology, even for a humble gardener!

I believe that the most useful thing gardeners can do, when it comes to managing their plot, is to have a wild element within their garden.

There is a lot of new information in the public domain about gardening without chemicals. The catalyst was the EU Pesticides Review (1992–2009), set up to address environmental concerns and to reduce the incidence of expensive litigation against certain chemical companies. The review began by identifying 900 existing active substances used in horticulture, and each one had to be supported by a comprehensive data package (or dossier) that met the requirements of the directive. Many companies failed to complete a dossier and as a result over 500 substances were withdrawn from the EU market. This slow process prompted a great deal of academic research into how to manage crops in a new age where fewer chemicals were available. Chemical-free pest control in horticulture and agriculture was explored and much of this is useful to the gardener. Where possible, I've included it.

Predated snail shells come in many forms. This one's been neatly drilled by something

THE DREADED GASTROPOD

-9-
THE DREADED GASTROPOD

One of the hardest things to explain to fellow gardeners is that I don't have masses of problems with slugs or snails. When I'm doing a talk on my garden this declaration is met with complete incredulity, sometimes expressed with great feeling! At other times eyes will roll back into their sockets, or startled eyebrows will make a sudden jerk up towards the ceiling, or I'll just get 'hard eye', heavy sighing or murmurs of disbelief.

In short, they don't believe me and so when it comes to questions, I often get a mauling. One gentleman told me I'd skated over slugs, implying that I hadn't mentioned them enough, and the imp within me exclaimed that we've all skated over slugs. Someone will inevitably mention the loss of two trays of bedding plants, no doubt plucked from the garden centre and planted on the very same day. These soft, sappy offerings had disappeared by next morning and the gardeners taken it very personally, as if a thief had stolen knickers from their washing line. Lots of these losses could be avoided by hardening off young plants – putting them somewhere airy for a few days to toughen up the foliage.

One year all my dahlias were ravaged and on another occasion all my annual cosmos were reduced to stumps.

I'm not immune to losing plants myself! One year all my dahlias were ravaged and on another occasion all my annual cosmos were reduced to stumps. Both failed to recover. In response, I stopped growing dahlias in mixed borders close to snail catchers such as kniphofias and hemerocallis, and instead created a cutting garden and planted a dedicated dahlia bed on my allotment. I carried on growing cosmos in my rose and peony borders, but grew them on into larger plants and planted them later in the season. In other words, I changed strategies. Every year *Dictamnus albus* gets cropped off at Spring Cottage because the box topiary nearby is a refuge for slugs and snails. Trying to marry both just doesn't work, although I do keep trying.

The distinctive trail of the snail – rather like dashes of Morse code. Slugs produce a continuous trail

My raised beds are very high-sided and slugs are more prevalent here than anywhere else

When the inevitable furore over my lack of slugs dies down, I then confess that I do have a slug and snail problem in one area of my garden: on four high-sided raised beds at the shadier, lower end. I've speculated that it might be the damp niche between the soil and the wooden edge providing the perfect home for snails and slugs. Or could it be that the creatures that devour most of my slugs and snails in other parts of the garden can't scale the 22 cm (9 in) wall created by the high wooden sides. Frogs, toads and hedgehogs may not have enough Chris Bonington or Edmund Hillary spirit to climb the vertical precipice.

It's a conundrum, because it's very hard to say what does eat slugs. There's no tell-tale shell, as there is with the snail. Many gardeners resort to blue metaldehyde slug pellets, but then the very creatures that feed on slugs (beetles, amphibians, hedgehogs, etc.) are less likely to visit and thrive in your garden because the supply of slugs and snails they rely on disappears. A lack of predators will, in turn, encourage more slugs and snails.

I firmly believe that my slugs and snails are being heavily predated, and this is borne out partly by the number of snail shells found that are either empty, smashed or distressed.

SLUG PELLETS

Although I don't use pellets, and never have, some 400 billion slug pellets are sprinkled onto British gardens annually in order to protect sensitive plants. These blue pellets are also used commercially, and quantities are monitored in agriculture and horticulture. In 2000 they were applied to 930,743 hectares (just under 2.3 million acres) of land, a weight of 362,690 kg (356 imperial tons). In 2014, 944,278 hectares (just over 2.3 million acres) of land were treated, a total weight of 116,925 kg (115 imperial tons), according to the Pesticide Usage Survey Group. This reduction was due to restraints applied in 2013. The average percentage of metaldehyde, the active ingredient in these pellets, varies from 3 per cent in amateur products (the ones gardeners use) to 6 per cent in commercial applications used on farmers' fields.

The Pesticides Usage Survey shows that areas treated were similar in 2000 and 2014, although there was a slight increase in 2014. The difference in weight varies from year to year and possibly correlates to there being heavier rainfall in some years.

Metaldehyde is listed as highly toxic by inhalation, moderately toxic by ingestion and slightly toxic by dermal absorption. It acts on slugs – which are lured to the pellets by their cereal content – by inducing excessive secretion of mucus after it has been eaten, leading to subsequent dehydration and death. At high temperatures of around 20°C the activity of metaldehyde is optimised; at low temperatures its toxic effect may be diminished. The charity Pesticides Action Research UK (www.pan-uk.org) has a useful website.

THE METALDEHYDE PROBLEM

Metaldehyde is very motile in damp conditions, so it soon leaches into water courses, and at the moment there is no known way of extracting it from drinking water. According to the Environment Agency (EA), between 2009 and 2011 concentrations of metaldehyde were found in 81 of 647 (that is one in eight) of reservoirs, rivers and groundwaters in England and Wales from which drinking water is sourced.

Metaldehyde is very motile in damp conditions, so it soon leaches into water courses, and at the moment there is no known way of extracting it from drinking water.

Wet years encourage slugs and increase the use of metaldehyde pellets, so the problem will vary from year to year depending on weather. Following the wet summer of 2012, metaldehyde levels were above the standard recommended in many areas. In summer 2013, Natural England and the EA recorded that homes in Essex and Suffolk, drawing supplies from the River Stour, had to drink tap water containing a hundred times the recommended level of 0.1ppb! As a result, Drinking Water Safeguard Zones were introduced by the EA and the Drinking Water Inspectorate (DWI) to tackle the problems of contamination, including pesticide use and disposal. It's not a happy thought, and the various findings have prompted environmentalists to call for greater use of natural predators in place of chemicals. Voluntary restrictions have been put in place by the Health and Safety Executive (HSE) and applications during wet weather are discouraged. However, if levels continue to build, metaldehyde will almost certainly be banned in the UK unless a way of removing it from drinking water can be found. Research is ongoing.

EXCEEDING THE DOSE – ALL TOO EASY

Many gardeners sprinkle slug pellets far too liberally, partly due to their being sold relatively cheaply in large containers that have very wide necks. The RSPB recommends that individual pellets should be placed 10–15 cm (4–6 in) apart around the plant and not piled up in groups, but they tumble out easily when tipped.

DEADLY RESULTS – NOT ONLY FOR SLUGS

Metaldehyde is toxic to game, wild birds and animals, including dogs and cats, and is harmful to fish and other aquatic life.

The pellets are coloured blue to deter birds and the colour lingers far longer than the metaldehyde. The cereal in the pellets that lures the slugs also contains an olfactory repellent (Bitrex) which, when fresh, deters mammals; but this does fade, making the pellets particularly dangerous to dogs, which are attracted to the high cereal content. The RSPCA cite it as the most common known cause of dog deaths in cases referred to the Veterinary Poisons Information Service (VPIS). A retrospective analysis of telephone enquiries to the VPIS between 1985 and 2010 found 772 cases with follow-up showing suspected metaldehyde slug bait ingestion in dogs. Half the enquiries occurred between May and July, which is when slug bait is in peak use. Fatal outcomes ensued in 16 per cent of the 762 cases for which data were available. That's 122 dog fatalities caused by heaps of pellets.

It's extremely difficult to assess whether predators of slugs, such as hedgehogs, are harmed, because

> ## GOLDEN RULE
> Avoid using slug pellets because they also kill detritus-eating larger slugs and snails. Target small slugs and snails by picking them off plants and destroying them and them alone.

metaldehyde is rapidly metabolised. Any evidence tends to be anecdotal. It's said that hedgehogs suffering from slug-pellet poisoning show symptoms of disorientation, drunkenness and dehydration, and are sometimes seen wandering aimlessly in the open during the day. However, tests have shown that hedgehogs have eaten slugs killed by metaldehyde without noticeable effects, although generally they avoid them.

The question is, would a hungry hedgehog eat the pellets once the off-putting smell wore off?

The question is, would a hungry hedgehog eat the pellets once the off-putting smell wore off? I simply cannot say. I know that my garden always has a hedgehog or two. I see their droppings on the grass and I hear them snuffling in the evenings. I even have a daytime roost and, every year, I find one hibernating and have to cover it back up again. I like to think it's the untainted food supply, along with the wilder areas, that keeps them in my garden. (For more on hedgehogs, see Chapter 10.)

METHIOCARB

Although this has never been available as a garden product, until recently it was widely used on arable fields. The pellets, which are also dyed blue, are roughly ten times more toxic than metaldehyde and contain a cholinesterase carbamate compound which affects the nervous system. The pellets make the slugs swell up and die.

Methiocarb breaks down slowly and has been proved to have hazardous effects on grain-eating farm birds such as sparrows and finches. Rodents are also affected. It's also an insecticide, meaning it kills off many insects, including the friendly slug-eating beetle and the beneficial earthworm. In other words, it sees off your natural predators as well as your slugs (which may explain why slugs are such a problem for farmers). As a result, an EU ban has come into effect and all methiocarb pellets had to be used by 19 September 2015. Since that date it has been illegal to hold any stock of methiocarb.

FERRIC PHOSPHATE

Ferric phosphate quickly causes slugs to stop feeding. They become less mobile and die within 3–6 days, often underground so evidence of dead slugs cannot always be seen. This leads gardeners to believe that the pellets aren't working – and they may be correct, for many get eaten by rats because they do not contain Bitrex, the bitter additive used in metaldehyde.

GROUNDBREAKING NEW RESEARCH

One area of research on slugs on arable fields done for the Pesticides Review gave me an insight into the problems I have with slugs on my raised beds at Spring Cottage. It was found that environmentally managed fields – i.e. those not chemically treated – contained fewer slugs than conventionally managed fields that had been sprayed with pesticides and herbicides. This difference was discovered to be due to a greater incidence of large carabid beetles, or ground beetles, in the organic fields. Carabid beetles, both the adults and the larvae, devour slugs at every stage. There are now grants for wildflower strips and beetle banks for this very reason. Lots of information on slugs can be found at www.xerces.org/wp-content/uploads/2012/04/forest-land-management-and-mollusks.pdf.

> *Carabid beetles, both the adults and the larvae, devour slugs at every stage.*

In one agricultural study 2,000 beetles, all *Pterostrichus melanarius*, were captured in an oilseed rape field. They had consumed gastropods. The highest numbers of beetles congregated where the incidence of slugs was highest, so they were definitely targeting slug populations both as adults and larvae. The only two prey eaten in this study were the grey garden or grey field slug (*Deroceras reticulatum*) and the hedgehog slug (*Arion intermedius*): both are small, measuring up to 2 cm (¾ in) in length. In 2002 Professor William Symondson of Cardiff University and colleagues published research in the journal *Ecology* demonstrating that predation, again by *P. melanarius*, prevented slug populations from reaching pest status. This large, all-black beetle is widespread and common throughout the UK in gardens, grassland and farmland. (For more information on beetles, see pages 199–206.)

I believe that most of my garden has high populations of beetles, encouraged by the planting style and toxin-free environment. However, the high-sided raised beds do not seem to have many beetles, which may explain why they have more slugs.

THE GOOD, THE BAD AND THE UGLY

Slug pellets kill every slug and snail, and I certainly don't want to kill all my slugs *per se*, because some, such as *Arion ater* (the large black slug), prefer a diet of rotting vegetation, fungi, manure and even the odd decomposing dead

Large black slug (*Arion ater*)

animal. When rose petals fall, for instance, or the tulip finally drops its languid petals, I have often seen large black slugs hoover them up for me. These recyclers are very valuable to the gardener, so as wildlife presenter Bill Oddie once said, 'If it's big and black put it back.' Slightly confusing, though, because some closely allied species are reddish in colour. The only way to tell is to dissect their genitalia – now there's a thought!

There are 43 species of slugs in Britain, although only 18 are truly native. Many are not found in gardens, a fact backed up by Jennifer Owen's observations about her suburban Leicestershire garden, where she found only seven species in her 30-year study. However, one of the authors of the excellent *Slugs of Britain and Ireland: Identification, Understanding and Control*, recorded 14 species in his own garden.

It's the smallest slugs that do the most damage, and the three main villains are:

Netted or grey field slug (*Deroceras reticulatum*)
This small slug, measuring between 3 cm and 5 cm (up to 2 in), has a light fawn body with a chain of darker veins and blotches. Its soft, glistening body looks almost as though it has been through a car wash owing to the abundant milky mucus – which is a deterrent to predators. This is the plump, pinkish

ORGANIC STRATEGIES FOR ENCOURAGING SLUG PREDATORS

- Create undisturbed areas on the outer edges of your garden, because this will encourage ground beetles. They are the most effective predator.

- Plant densely in the borders to create shady cover. This will help your beetles to thrive.

- Target key areas of your garden by watering on nematodes. Late April is considered the optimum time. The soil needs to be warm and damp, so apply them in late afternoon when the soil is moist. The minimum temperature is critical, or you can waste a lot of money. Repeat if needed.

- Go out at dusk, wearing large boots rather than open-toed sandals, pick slugs off plants with your gloved fingers and squash them. Slug slime is almost impossible to remove from the fingers, so gloves are not just for the squeamish. Blackbirds often drag their slugs across the grass to remove the horrible, foul-tasting slime before tackling them.

- Slugs are cannibalistic. If you kill some slugs or snails at dusk, more will arrive to feast on the first lot, providing two opportunities for carnage.

- Plant decoy plants to lure your slugs away from vulnerable plants such as runner beans. The two most useful sacrificial plants are single-flowered French marigolds (*Tagetes patula*) and young lettuce plants.

- Harden your plants off if they've been in a greenhouse. Or grow them on so they are mature – a strategy that works well with dahlias.

- Hoe problem areas throughout the year to expose slug eggs. Birds will eat them and slugs are not at all happy in disturbed soil. The hostas at Highgrove, HRH the Prince of Wales's organic Gloucestershire garden, are kept clean partly owing to regular hoeing between the plants.

- Hoe vegetables regularly. If you disturb the top 10 cm (4 in) of soil it will prevent a lot of problems and it will also create a fine tilth above the soil. This mulch-like layer preserves moisture.

- Avoid mulching with moisture-trapping grass clippings or polythene. If you have to mulch strawberries with straw, for instance, remove it as quickly as you can after cropping.

- Tidy areas in autumn by removing old cabbage stumps, fading rhubarb foliage and other spent foliage. This will get rid of damp hiding places.

- Remove leaf-litter close to sensitive plants, but leave it intact where you can. Remember it's the insect duvet of the natural world.

- Avoid nitrogen-rich, fast-fix fertilisers that produce lots of sappy, new growth. Use slow-release fertilisers with balanced nutrients, such as Vitax Q4 which has 5.3 per cent nitrogen, 7.5 per cent phosphorus pentoxide and 10 per cent potassium oxide, plus 3 per cent magnesium oxide with trace elements.

- If you've had severe slug problems in spring and summer, make sure that debris is cleared and do a thorough tidy where you can before winter sets in.

The slimy grey field slug (*Deroceras reticulatum*) is the one you find in lettuces!

slug found in your hearting lettuces and cabbages. It feeds mostly on seeds and plants above ground, but it's a problem because it continues to be active in damp weather and even when temperatures are close to freezing. Breeding is generally at a peak in April and May and then again from September to October. However, in favourable conditions the grey field slug will breed throughout the year. In optimum conditions *D. reticulatum* can start to lay eggs within 16 weeks of hatching.

Garden slug (*Arion hortensis* group)

This group, which consists of *Arion hortensis*, *A. owenii* and *A. distinctus*, are known as roundback slugs and they have wrinkled backs and no raised keel (prominent ridge on its back). They are larger than the grey field slug, typically 2.5–3.5 cm (around 1–1.5 in). The body is dark and the foot (underside) ranges from yellow to orange. All the species in this group produce characteristic yellow-orange mucus and, like all *Arion* species, they are active only at temperatures above 5°C. They live for one year only.

Common keeled slug (*Tandonia budapestensis*)

This is the dark brownish-grey or almost black slug that penetrates your potatoes

SLUG FACTS

- All slug species are hermaphrodite (i.e. each individual is both male and female). While some species are self-fertile, most mate before laying eggs in batches of 10–50 in soil cavities, between clods, under stones or at the base of plants.

- Up to 500 eggs per slug may be laid over several weeks. Eggs develop slowly in the winter, but will hatch within a few weeks when the temperature starts to rise.

- In their lifetime, slugs will travel only a few metres from their hatching site, in a circular route, in search of food. So if you don't fancy jumping on them, take them for a long walk.

These facts are drawn from the Agriculture and Horticulture Development Board's Information Sheet 02.

and root crops. If seen, it is usually curled into a sickle shape, but most of the time it's invisible because it's underground. It has a keel (or ridge) and a clearly visible yellow line along its body. Keeled slugs (*Milax*, *Tandonia* and *Boettgerilla* species) are more or less subterranean, coming to the surface only during the breeding season.

SNAILS

Snails can cause the gardener just as much heartbreak as slugs do, because they can feed throughout the day in damp conditions. They glide up and down iris foliage, and hide in kniphofias and hemerocallis on damp days. However, they are not active in cold weather. They seal their shells up and some cluster together, whilst others overwinter on their own, so it's always a good idea to investigate nooks and crannies in winter, such as the backs of drainpipes or under the lips of pots. There are 99 species of land snail in Britain, and about half of them are common and widespread. About 20 have been introduced by

This pot contained over 70 hibernating common garden snails – until I found them!

man, including the common garden snail (*Cornu aspersum*). This scientific name has changed several times and older books will refer to it as *Helix aspersa* or *Cantareus aspersus*.

As with slugs, there are not likely to be many species in your garden. Jennifer Owen found eight species of land snail in her garden over 30 years and these are all widespread and common. They were: the common garden snail and the strawberry snail (*Trichia striolata*), as well as four species of glass snail – the small pale *Vitrea contracta*, the smooth glass snail *Aegopinella nitidula*, a larger species named *Oxychilus draparnaudi* and the garlic glass snail *Oxychilus alliarius*. She also found the great pond snail (*Lymnaea stagnalis*) and the ramshorn snail (*Planorbis planorbis*) in her pond.

> **GOLDEN RULE**
>
> There are plenty of slug and snail resistant plants that you could use, and those that are sought out by slugs can be used as slug magnets – for easier collection and dispatch!

We have glass snails at Spring Cottage, but keying out the species is beyond me. We also get the white-lipped snail (*Cepaea hortensis*) and the brown-lipped snail (*Cepaea nemoralis*). Neither of these, although abundant here, is recorded in Owen's study. We almost certainly also have the copse snail (*Arianta arbustorum*), a medium-sized brown snail, although we haven't found any shells as yet.

Snails have a simple lifecycle. Most species lay eggs although some are ovoviviparous, the eggs hatching inside the mother. Larger species may lay clutches of 50–200 eggs, but the smaller species lay fewer and some of them lay single eggs. Most can breed at any time of the year except in the depths of winter, so eggs, juveniles and adults can be found at almost any time. Newly hatched snails look like tiny versions of the adult, and grow by adding whorls to their shell. As the juvenile nears adulthood it lays down a lip around the mouth of the shell, often decorated with ridges and prominences, and ceases to add whorls. Adults, therefore, have a final size and do not continue to get bigger throughout their lives.

Snails have a simple lifecycle. Most species lay eggs although some are ovoviviparous, the eggs hatching inside the mother.

Shells contain a lot of calcium carbonate, so calcium is a very important part of the diet. The greatest diversity of snails is found on calcium-rich soils; acid soils may have no snails at all. Some species have been badly affected by pollution such as acid rain, but de-industrialisation and legislation means that many cities, particularly in the north of England, are being recolonised. Most species live for less than a year, although the larger species may take two or more years to reach adulthood.

In spring and early summer, thrushes devour many snails

MY SNAIL SHELLS

Although it's almost impossible to track the end of a slug, because the whole thing has probably been consumed leaving little visible evidence behind, I find plenty of snail shells at Spring Cottage in various conditions. Some have been heavily pecked to reveal the coiled inner nautilus, and this may be rats. Others have been drilled into, leaving a small hole, and this is mystifying. Some are empty, but undamaged, and these may have been predated by beetle larvae. We often find clusters of completely empty shells in the same place year after year, and perhaps this is a small rodent. One of our caches is right by the stone wall close to the lavabo – the Roman wash basin built into our low stone wall and now cemented in.

We also find completely smashed snail shells near stones, and these are the handiwork of the thrush (*Turdus philomelos*). This bird finds a suitably large snail and holds it in its beak, by the rim of the shell aperture, then beats it repeatedly against a handy stone, or 'anvil'. Usually, a section of the shell eventually breaks free and the snail's body is extracted through the hole. A song thrush never uses its feet to help. The whole process can take several minutes and they mostly go for the larger common garden snail. Sometimes we can hear the thrushes bashing the snails and find the remnants of shell left behind on the anvil stone.

We often find clusters of completely empty shells in the same place year after year, and perhaps this is a small rodent.

The song thrush is the only European member of its family to use an anvil to break open snails. Its relatives the redwing (*T. iliacus*) and fieldfare (*T. pilaris*), both of which are winter visitors to many British gardens, also take snails, but

SLUG AND SNAIL PROOF PLANTS

The RHS lists the following slug- and snail-resistant plants:

Acanthus mollis (bear's breeches)

Achillea filipendulina

Agapanthus hybrids and cultivars

Alchemilla mollis (lady's mantle)

Anemone × hybrida and *A. hupehensis* (Japanese anemone)

Antirrhinum majus (snapdragon)

Aquilegia species

Armeria species

Aster amellus, A.× frikartii,(Michaelmas daisies)

Astilbe × arendsii

Astrantia major

Bergenia (elephant's ears)

Centaurea dealbata, C. montana

Corydalis lutea

Cynara cardunculus (globe artichoke)

Dicentra spectabilis (bleeding heart)

Digitalis purpurea (foxglove)

Eryngium species

Euphorbia species (spurges)

Foeniculum vulgare (fennel)

Fuchsia cultivars

Gaillardia aristata

Geranium species

Geum chiloense

Hemerocallis cultivars (day lilies)

Papaver nudicaule (Iceland poppy)

Pelargonium

Phlox paniculata

Physostegia virginiana (obedient plant)

Polemonium foliosissimum

Polygonum species

Potentilla hybrids and cultivars

Pulmonaria species (lungwort)

Rudbeckia fulgida

Salvia × superba

Saxifraga × urbium (London pride)

Scabiosa caucasica (scabious)

Sedum spectabile (ice plant)

Sempervivum species (houseleeks)

Sisyrinchium species

Solidago species (golden rod)

Stachys macrantha

Symphyotrichum cultivars and species

Tanacetum coccineum (pyrethrum)

Thalictrum aquilegiifolium

Tradescantia virginiana

Tropaeolum species (nasturtium)

Verbascum species (mullein)

Astrantias do not attract slugs

Predated snail shells vary enormously. Some are heavily eaten – perhaps by female birds about to lay eggs. Others have neatly drilled holes

generally they either swallow them whole or extract the body by beating the animal against the ground. The blackbird (*T. merula*) occasionally takes snails itself, but is more often seen robbing the song thrush of its hard-earned food.

Sometimes the shells of the snails I find have definitely been eaten, because no fragments remain nearby. Female birds need extra calcium during the breeding season, for egg laying, so more snails seem to be eaten in late winter and early spring than at other times of the year. A study of female great tits (*Parus major*) undertaken in the Netherlands showed that they prefer to ingest partly degraded and therefore brittle empty shells. Presumably the calcium from these is more easily assimilated, so it's quite likely that female birds, including blue tits (*Cyanistes*

> *Sometimes the shells of the snails I find have definitely been eaten, because no fragments remain nearby.*

STRATEGIES FOR DEALING WITH SNAILS

- Seek them out in winter and destroy them if you find them.

- Frisk leafy plants, such as kniphofias, hemerocallis and evergreen eryngiums in spring.

- Leave 9 cm (3 in) plastic pots in the border, laying them on their sides. These will trap snails.

- If you see them, squash them but leave the remnants around as slugs will devour them – allowing for a double hit.

- Hoe close to plants and expose the eggs. They will dry out, or be eaten by birds and other predators.

caeruleus), are targeting empty shells purely for extra calcium rather than the meaty contents.

The best estimate we have of the effect of predation by the song thrush on snail populations is that it is responsible for 12–25 per cent of winter mortality in both the copse snail and the white-lipped snail. This figure falls to less than 1 per cent in summer. I had far more thrushes in my Hook Norton garden and they predated garden snails in great numbers during the 1990s, so much so that the paths were crunchy underfoot in summer.

It's quite likely that female birds, are targeting empty shells purely for extra calcium

The present garden in Cold Aston has far fewer thrushes, but the thrush has declined overall. There is more on this in Chapter 10 (page 145).

A small tortoiseshell butterfly on buddleia

THE FLYING SQUAD

-10-
THE FLYING SQUAD

Most creatures that fly and visit flowers pollinate and outcross by taking pollen from one flower to another. This is a vital process needed to produce seeds and fruit. If pollinators didn't do the job we would have to get a paintbrush out, because very few plants are self-fertile. In south-west China the wild bees have been almost eradicated by excessive pesticide use and the loss of their natural habitat, so apple and pear crops have to be pollinated by hand. The farmers carry pots of pollen and paintbrushes and individually pollinate every flower. Apparently they get their children to climb up to the highest blossoms – but they won't be as good as the bees! Bee expert Dave Goulson, writing in 2012 on the website Chinadialogue, points out that 'there are not enough humans in the world to pollinate all of our crops by hand'.

In America they ferry in hives of honeybees to pollinate almond blossom, etc. However, colony collapse disorder, thought to be caused by continual pesticide use, is making this a precarious business, because the bees fail to return to the hive and the colony dies. America's Natural Resources Defence Council records that '42 per cent of U.S. bee colonies collapsed in 2015, well above the average 31 per cent that have been dying each winter for nearly a decade. This devastating decline is due in large part to the skyrocketing use of dangerous pesticides called neonicotinoids, or "neonics", unleashed by multinational chemical giants like Bayer, Monsanto, and Syngenta.'

It's not rocket science. We need to sustain healthy insect pollinators because they are vital to both our wellbeing and the planet's. Gardeners are in a good position to help because eco-friendly gardens do get more pollinators. I get great delight here in watching them.

In this section I've picked out some of my most helpful pollinators. Many also contribute to pest control.

A honeybee feeding on *Sedum spectabile*

Nectar-rich plants, such as *Crocosmia* 'Lucifer' are adored by social wasps and for most of the year these wasps predate small creatures too

WASPS

SOCIAL WASPS

The most noticeable wasps are the social wasps, the ones that build papery nests by scraping slivers of wood from your garden shed, your best garden furniture or, in our case, our ornamental chestnut gates. In our time at Spring Cottage we've had wasp nests in the roof and in the laurel hedge right by these gates. The one in the laurel hedge blew down and proved to be an intricate work of art, one that any architect would be proud of. It was grey and silvery in colour. Every sliver of wood has to be masticated, or chewed up, to form a papery substance, although we are not sure which species built it.

There are eight species of social wasp in the UK, distinguished mostly by the arrangement of black markings on their yellow faces and abdomens.

There are eight species of social wasp in the UK, distinguished mostly by the arrangement of black markings on their yellow faces and abdomens.

The common wasp (*Vespula vulgaris*) and the German wasp (*V. germanica*) are both found in gardens. They're very similar in appearance, with black and yellow stripes, but the best way to tell them apart is to look at the dots on the abdomen. The German wasp has black dots between the bands, whereas the dots on the common wasp are fused into the black bands on the abdomen. Markings on the face also vary. The common wasp has an anchor-shaped marking rather than the dots or vertical strip on the German wasp. The eyes also vary, and the German wasp has a complete yellow band behind the eye. It's tricky telling them apart in the garden, unless you find a dead one, because both measure 12–17 mm (½ in) in length. In flight, it is impossible to tell the difference.

A wasp's nest in a neighbour's laurel hedge

You may also see a European hornet (*Vespa crabro*), another larger social wasp measuring up to 30 mm (over 1 in) long. I sometimes see these in warm summers, and they are more common in the warmer, southern half of Britain; they weren't found in Jennifer Owen's Leicestershire study, for instance. The hornet has a fearful reputation, quite unfounded in my own experience, because these gentle giants aren't aggressive when visiting my garden. There's been no evidence that they've nested in the garden, but I have seen them on drizzly days paying attention to the standard gooseberries. They seem immune to the weather.

I am a great supporter of these social wasps because they are brilliant predators for much of the year, taking their prey back to the nest to feed their brood. The workers, always females, will catch flies, aphids, butterfly and moth caterpillars, sawfly larvae and other invertebrates, making them an important insect-controlling predator.

I watched in awe one day after spotting huge cabbage white caterpillars nibbling the foliage of my white sea stock, *Matthiola incana*. These grow right under the study window and their white flowers scent the path up to the front door, so these plants, which are members of the Brassica family, are highly precious to me. I also get caterpillars on other ornamental members of the brassica family, such as sweet rocket (*Hesperis matronalis*), although I don't mind that so much. The cabbage white caterpillars on my white sea stock were already fat and juicy, and I know that when they get that large they are rarely eaten by anything because they are full of mustard oil absorbed from the brassica leaves. This makes them unpalatable and even my chickens, normally so voracious, walk away. As I looked on and tutted, I noticed a wasp or two, and then a pack of four homed in on one caterpillar and started to slice it into sections. It took several minutes, but finally they flew off with the pieces. I was mesmerised, and when I came back later that day the caterpillars were all missing. It taught me the value of the social wasp! I despair when I see wasp traps in garden centres, because wasps spend the first part of the year collecting protein-rich food – things we regard as pests – for the larvae, so it's best to think of them as meat-eating bees.

> *When cabbage white caterpillars get large they are rarely eaten by anything because they are full of mustard oil absorbed from the Brassica leaves.*

GOLDEN RULE

Mix up the colours and the flower shapes in your garden. Avoid using lots of double petal-packed blooms.

Wasps only turn to sugar for food later in the year and understanding their lifecycle helps to explain why. They follow a similar lifecycle to bumblebees. The large queens hibernate through the winter, emerging in late spring to top up on energy-rich nectar and protein-rich pollen. The queen begins to build a cylindrical column, known as a petiole, and this is covered by a chemical produced by the queen which repels ants. Next she produces a single hexagonal cell and surrounds it with a further six hexagonal

Kniphofia 'Prince Igor' has so much nectar, if you knock it, it showers you in sweet liquid

cells. She continues building until she has 20–30 cells and then lays an egg in each. Once the eggs have hatched she divides her time between feeding the larvae and more nest building. The full-size larvae spin a cover over their cell and stay there until they have developed into adult workers. (For further information, see the conservation charity Buglife's website: www.buglife.org.uk.)

Once the workers have emerged, they hunt for protein-rich insects to take back to the nest to feed the rest of the larvae – so the larvae are fed on insects from your garden. The workers are rewarded with a small, sugar-rich droplet of liquid saliva produced by the larvae. This sugary fix is abundant when the nest contains many larvae, but gets harder to find once there are more adults than larvae. By late summer, when there are no or few larvae left, the adult wasp begins to look for alternative sugar fixes in your garden, or your kitchen.

I get round this problem by planting August-flowering plants that are full of nectar. My *Kniphofia* 'Prince Igor' is one of their favourites because, should you knock up against it, it will shower your arm with sugary nectar. Wasps flock to it, disappearing within the flowers, and they also enjoy crocosmias. You could also grow native figwort (*Scrophularia nodosa*), a plant largely pollinated by wasps.

SOLITARY WASPS

The vast majority of the 9,000 or so species of wasp in the UK do not live in colonies like the social wasp. They are solitary creatures. Some provision nests they have dug with insect food, whilst others – known as parasitic wasps (see page 153) – lay their eggs inside living insects.

Some solitary wasps are found in gardens, although some are so tiny they can barely be seen without a microscope. They rarely have common names, but Jennifer Owen recorded 55 species, divided into six families, and she trapped some 3,610 in her 30-year study. They were not as abundant as her solitary bees, though, which numbered 6,686. She also says that solitary wasps were 'rarely evident in the garden'.

Most solitary wasps build a nest in the ground with a few cells and then pack the cells with suitable food, which they have paralysed rather than killed. This paralysed food lasts far longer than dead food, so it is edible for longer. The chosen food is often quite specific for each wasp. It may be aphids, spiders or beetles. Some wasps don't bother to collect their own, but devour the food supplies stored by other solitary wasps. Jennifer Owen's most commonly trapped solitary wasp (*Omalus auratus*), for example, raids the aphids and spiders stored by other solitary wasps. It's a bit like going to the supermarket for a ready-meal rather than doing your own cooking.

We noticed a black and shiny solitary wasp, name unknown, in the cracks of the paving right by our front door, because it was darting out to catch spiders. It was very nervous and twitchy, and the sunlight caught its dark, almost metallic body. We were fascinated by its darting movement and hesitant manner. It dashed out and dragged a small spider into a crack between two flagstones. This was my first sighting of a spider-hunting wasp (*Pompilidae*), but there are 40 species in the UK. They provision each nest cell with one spider. At least one species bites the legs off its paralysed prey so it can carry it to the nest – probably sensible, because the spiders they catch are often larger than they are. Having seen one, we found another a few minutes later, this time on the steps up to the greenhouse.

Some solitary wasps are found in gardens, although some are so tiny they can barely be seen without a microscope.

We also get digger wasps in the garden, usually smaller and more delicate than social wasps and with more black than yellow. Buglife states that there are 110 species of digger wasp in Britain. As the name suggests, female digger wasps burrow into the ground when nesting, using spiny brushes on their legs. Their tunnels can go down almost 30 cm (1 ft) deep and have several branches. One egg is laid in each branch. Deeper holes provide more constant temperatures, which helps the eggs to develop and stores the food more securely. The hole is packed with paralysed prey – ready meals.

Here, digger wasps often lurk close to the nests of our ashy mining bees (see pages 161–3) and my thoughts are that the digger wasps are trying to save themselves some of the spade work by commandeering a mining bee's hole. There are often spoil heaps on the ground, tiny cones of soil with a hole at the top that resemble a child's idea of a volcano. We assume they've been made by our ashy mining bees, although it could be they're being added to by digger wasps.

Cotesia glomerata parasitising newly hatched cabbage white caterpillars

The caterpillar's body ruptures

The cocoons overwinter and the new adults emerge in spring to repeat the cycle

PARASITIC WASPS

There are 6,000 species of parasitic wasps and they account for the greatest proportion of Hymenoptera in Britain. Many are incredibly small and almost ant-like, so it's difficult to collect them, identify them and study them and as a result little is known about many. Jeremy Early's book, *My Side of the Fence*, and website (see page 242) provides an excellent resource. The adults generally lay eggs inside a host, and some parasitic wasps are so useful that they are being reared and can be purchased for the biological control of certain glasshouse pests – for instance, *Encarsia forma* is used for glasshouse whitefly and *Aphidius* species for aphids. The Braconid wasp (*Spathius exarator*) can remove up to 90 per cent of a woodworm (*Anobium punctatum*) infestation.

Most parasitic wasps develop as larvae inside the larval or nymphal stages of insects or other invertebrate animals. Some attack the pupal stage and a few feed inside the bodies of adult insects. Some female parasitic wasps have a long, sting-like egg-laying structure on the rear end of the abdomen. This is particularly true of parasites whose prey lives in a concealed situation, such as inside a plant stem. During the early stages of the parasite's development it causes no obvious harm to the host animal. The host carries on feeding and growing. However, in the later stages of the parasite's development it destroys its host's vital organs and kills it.

Caterpillars of the large cabbage white butterfly are parasitised by *Cotesia glomerata* as the larvae hatch from the eggs. The caterpillars carry on eating, unfortunately for your cabbage crop, but eventually their bodies rupture to reveal sulphur-yellow silk cocoons.

Good books on wildlife gardening are rarities, but I can thoroughly recommend Jeremy Early's *My Side of the Fence*, mentioned above. He is the chairman of the Bees, Wasps and Ants Recording Society (BWARS) and a trustee of the charity Hymettus (www.hymettus.org.uk), which funds extensive research into British invertebrates, chiefly bees, wasps and ants (www.natureconservationimaging.com). Jeremy has a fascinating chapter on wasps, with pictures of them and their prey. His Surrey garden saw '77 species of wasp turn up, with at least 28 nesting. Half of them were nationally rare or scarce, and were only found in less than ten per cent of the two kilometre squares used for recording in Surrey.' Jennifer Owen's Leicestershire study found 23 rare species. Both of these are evidence that eco-friendly gardens make good habitats and will, and do, attract rarities, many of which the gardener will never notice owing to their size.

> *Eco-friendly gardens make good habitats and will, and do, attract rarities.*

BEES

I always greatly enjoy watching bees going about their pollination duties. Some bees have pollen baskets and the colour of the pollen can change from yellow to orange; I've even seen a turquoise-blue pollen sac, presumably from bees visiting *Dianthus cruentus*, a species pink with vivid blue stamens. Insect-pollinated plants produce stickier pollen, so many bees with furry bodies carry lots of it on their heads and bodies. Some, like the leafcutter bee, have a pollen-laden underside. Tongue length varies in bees, so they all have their flower preferences, and in the plant directory I've picked out some favourites – see Chapter 12.

BUMBLEBEES

Bumblebees are far more noticeable than most types of wasp. We have 24 species in Britain according to the Bumblebee Conservation Trust, the charity established by Dave Goulson (see pages 9–10) to flag up the fact that bumblebee populations have crashed within the last eighty or so years. Two species have become nationally extinct, 15 others have declined or contracted, and this is still ongoing.

Gardeners can expect to see up to eight species in their gardens, and one of the most important things is to provide a source of nectar early in the year, for some queen bees can emerge from hibernation in late January and February if the temperature reaches 10°C. The winter of 2015/2016 was extremely clement and I saw buff-tailed queen bees (*Bombus terrestris*) out between Christmas and New Year. Luckily there were hellebores, some pulmonarias and several flowering shrubs to sustain them. Flying uses up a lot of energy, so if they can't find nectar the queen bees are likely to die.

> *Gardeners can expect to see up to eight species in their gardens.*

Bombus hypnorum, the tree bumblebee prefers simply shaped flowers that open flat (see page 82)

Five species of bumblebee thrive within the Arctic Circle because of this unique 'warm-up' technique.

Bumblebees are the only group of bees capable of flying in such low temperatures, and they manage to do so because of their unique ability to rev up their flight muscles chemically. Five species of bumblebee thrive within the Arctic Circle because of this unique 'warm-up' technique. Currants, broad beans, gooseberries and many fruit trees rely on these early foragers and would probably not succeed without them.

The large buff-tailed queens are usually the first bumblebees to emerge from hibernation, and in my old garden they tended to head straight for the winter-flowering clematis (*Clematis cirrhosa* var. *balearica*) situated on the south-facing wall. I could hear them bumping into the window in their 'almost-awake' state as they stumbled into the pale, maroon-spotted bells. The heavily spotted 'Freckles' or the plainer 'Wisley Cream' are also desirable; autumn is the perfect time to plant one of these early-flowering clematis. They all need a south-facing spot.

> *Many prefer to nest underground in abandoned rodent burrows, because digging is quite a task for bumblebees.*

Other species follow later in spring and, once the bumblebee queens have refreshed themselves on early nectar, they begin to feed on protein-rich pollen to stimulate their reproductive systems. Then they start to zigzag over the ground in search of new nesting sites. Many prefer to nest underground in abandoned rodent burrows, because digging is quite a task for bumblebees. Some use crevices in walls, others nest above ground in dead leaves or compost heaps. It can be quite inconvenient having a bees' nest in the compost heap, because it must remain undisturbed for several months, but it is good fun watching them.

New colonies are started early in the year and the first worker bees to emerge are small. As the colony becomes more successful, the bees reach full size. This seasonal differential makes identifying species difficult even with a good bee chart, and my first foray into identifying red-tailed bumblebees (*B. lapidarius*) was a complete flop because I went by size, not markings or the hairs on their legs. *B. lapidarius* likes stony sites, in my experience, and we had one nest in stone at the base of the study window, in a very warm, south-facing position. It was a delight watching them go in and out of their nest, but once a nest has been used it is normally not occupied again because it may contain parasites. In late August a fresh brood of pristine red-tailed queens emerged from our nest and gathered on nearby echinacea flowers for their first taste of summer nectar.

GOLDEN RULE

Provide habitat for insects. A grassy, sunny bank will often suffice.

POLLEN IS NOT ENOUGH

I have always felt that far too much weight is given to providing nectar and pollen, which is in abundant supply in most gardens in any case. Bumblebees also need nesting sites in sunny banks, under trees and in walls. The sight of a queen bee zigzagging over the ground is an exciting one, but you have to provide relatively untouched areas for nesting sites. In winter I am cautious about

Bumblebees are able to access flowers, such as this antirrhinum

White-tailed bumblebee (*Bombus lucorum*) on *Eryngium giganteum*

Tubular flowers are often popular with bumblebees

A nest made by *Osmia bicolor*. Underneath the foliage was an empty brown-lipped snail

----

Red-tailed Bumblebee (*Bombus lapidarius*)
Queens and workers have a distinctive black body with an orange-red tail. Males have distinct yellow facial hairs and a yellow band on the thorax, with a black abdomen and a bright orange-red tail. The hairs on the pollen baskets (on the hind legs) of the female are all black, but these may be red in males. Loves blue annual cornflowers (*Centaurea cyanus*). Widespread and generally common.

Buff-tailed bumblebee (*Bombus terrestris*)
Queens, workers and males have a dull golden-yellow collar near the head and a band on the abdomen. The queen's tail is an off-white to buff colour, which can sometimes appear orange. The workers have a white tail with a subtle buff line separating the tail from the rest of the abdomen. Unlike many species, the buff-tailed male's facial hair is black, as opposed to yellow. Males have a buff-tinged tail. Loves spring-flowering bulbs and eryngiums; also robs nectar from long-tubed flowers. The commonest bumblebee over lowland Britain.

White-tailed bumblebee (*Bombus lucorum*)
A showier bee, with brighter white markings and brighter yellow bands. The queens, workers and males have a yellow band on the thorax and on the abdomen. The males have yellow hair on their head, and extra tufts of yellow hair on the thorax and abdomen. Short-tongued, but robs nectar from comfrey and honeysuckle. Will feed on umbellifers. One of the commonest bees.

Garden bumblebee (*Bombus hortorum*)
Three yellow bands at the front and rear of the thorax and a third band at the front of the abdomen. The tail is a clean white colour. The face is distinctly long, differentiating it from other species with similar banding, such as the heath bumblebee (*B. jonellus*). It is a very long-tongued species and prefers flowers with deep tubes. Favourite flowers include bluebell, comfrey and dandelions in spring, followed by thistles, scabious and foxgloves. Widespread and generally common.

Early bumblebee (*Bombus pratorum*)
Queens, workers and males have a yellow band on the thorax and abdomen, although the abdominal yellow banding is less pronounced or missing in workers. The tail is often dark orange-red, which may fade with time, and is not anything like as vivid as the tail of the red-tailed bumblebee. They are also smaller in size, especially in springtime. Males have a broad yellow collar that wraps around the thorax, and yellow hair on the face. A short-tongued bee, which robs the nectar from comfrey but also visits raspberries, brambles and hardy geraniums. One of the commonest and most widespread species.

Common carder bee (*Bombus pascuorum*)
A gingery-looking bee, and the only common one in this colour range. Here it pollinates raspberry and currant flowers in spring. Prefers legumes, labiates, scabious, thistles and knapweeds. The commonest and most widespread bumblebee in the British Isles.

Tree bumblebee (*Bombus hypnorum*)
This small, clean-cut bumblebee was first recorded in Landford in Wiltshire in 2001, although we didn't see one here until 2007. It's now found over most of England, as far north as Carlisle, and throughout much of Wales, and has now been recorded in Scotland as well. Its ginger thorax, black abdomen and white tail, a unique combination, give it a very clean-cut appearance. It probably arrived from the Continent, and is also found in mainland Europe, through Asia and up into the Arctic Circle. These aerial nesters have been known to nest in bird boxes.

disturbing any clump of foliage that looks as though it has been glued together, because if I move it there's usually a hole underneath. It's probably a hibernating bee trying to keep the worst of the weather away, so I put the clump back if I happen to move it by accident.

WHY ARE BUMBLEBEES SO VITAL?

Bumblebees browse-pollinate from one flower species to another rather than selecting one type of flower and feeding from it again and again, as honeybees tend to. When I had a lowly post in a vegetable research lab, a hive of honeybees under netting failed to cross-pollinate two flowering varieties of Brussels sprouts despite the fact they looked identical to the human eye. They selected 'Peer Gynt' exclusively, ignoring the other variety completely, even though they were inter-planted. We had to bring in blowflies to complete the work, as they did not discriminate between the two varieties.

Some commercial glasshouses have mechanical vibrators to 'buzz-pollinate' their tomato crops, but I'd rather have the bees.

The bumblebee can also buzz-pollinate flowers, a unique attribute. It literally shakes the stubborn pollen down by buzzing inside the flower – something honeybees can't manage. Some plants (such as tomatoes and other members of the Solanum family) can only be pollinated in this way. Some commercial glasshouses have mechanical vibrators to 'buzz-pollinate' their tomato crops, but I'd rather have the bees.

Bumblebees also fly greater distances than other bees, travelling up to 2 miles in search of food. When you consider that 80 per cent of the world's food crops require a pollinator, it's vital to protect bees, and gardeners can really make a difference.

FLOWER COLOUR AND SHAPE

Colour and shape are important for pollinators, and different species have their preferences. Bees seem to be drawn to blue flowers and, as they pick up ultraviolet, any petals with veins or spots attract them, indicating that this plant is bee-friendly. Flies, which are excellent pollinators, like dull greens and whites, and often these flowers emit a meaty smell, as in *Helleborus foetidus*. Hoverflies often have small mouth parts, so flower heads that consist of tiny flowers, such as astrantias and cow-parsley-like flowers, are highly attractive to them. However, they are also drawn to orange flowers, so African marigolds and calendulas pull them in, as well.

Jennifer Owen was able to find eight species of bumblebee in her Leicestershire garden, one more than me, although she didn't record the tree bumblebee because it hadn't arrived in Leicestershire at that time. She trapped 86 ruderal or large garden bumblebees (*B. ruderatus*), but this has a more easterly and south-easterly range, albeit a sparse one. It is in serious decline. She also trapped 114 red-shanked carder bees (*B. ruderarius*), a black-bodied bee that I may have seen in my Spring Cottage garden. This is in substantial decline and indeed has died out in south-west England and in areas north of the Midlands. However, I think this may be the bee that visits my yellow rattle (*Rhinanthus minor*), although I rarely see it on anything else. I believe that our meadow flowers, mainly British natives, are bringing in more bumblebees.

> *I believe that our meadow flowers, mainly British natives, are bringing in more bumblebees.*

In the countryside, recent changes in farming practice have made a difference. When I walk down our lane, which leads to a farmhouse about a mile away, wide wildflower strips follow parts of the road. They've been there for three or four years now and, when the wildflowers are out, there are plenty of bees about. We also see beetles crossing the road now. Before these strips were in place, the farmer ploughed up to the track and we rarely saw any bees or insects. Five years ago the Best Beloved and I walked for 7 miles on a spring day in early April. We spotted seven bumblebees, mostly queens, during our afternoon ramble and equated it as one for every mile. The only wildflowers were a relict population of cowslips on the side of a hill. When we returned home we saw far more than that as we walked up our garden path. On another occasion we took a 4-mile late-spring walk in rather poor weather, spotting only four bumblebees, again one per mile.

GOLDEN RULE
Avoid pesticides in your own garden – they will affect the health of your bees.

SOLITARY BEES

There are more than 275 species of solitary bee in Britain, and over 90 per cent of them are not social and do not live in colonies. We see lots of solitary bees at Spring Cottage. Some resemble small wasps, others look like small bees and some look almost ant-like, to me anyway. Although they drink nectar, they spend most of their time collecting pollen, which they mix with a small amount of nectar. In the process, a lot of pollen gets attached to their bodies and stays there until it is brushed off on another flower. This makes them fantastic pollinators. It's said, for instance, that the red mason bee (*Osmia rufa*) is 120

The ashy mining bees make little volcanoes on the main lawn

A mining bee volcano

times more efficient at pollinating than a bumblebee. All solitary bees are non-aggressive and do not swarm, so the red mason bee is often used to pollinate commercial crops, including apples. Solitary bees do not produce wax, nor do they have a queen.

We have also had *O. bicolor*, the two-coloured mason bee, building an elaborate nest, by arranging sticks and leaves in an untidy bundle. This camouflaged a snail shell which had been covered in chewed material. We once watched one carrying improbably long pieces of grass as it flew back to its nest (see page 157).

MINING BEES

Seventy per cent of solitary bees are mining bees. Some of these rather hairy bees seem to be gregarious, if our lawn is anything to go by. We can watch as the whole area becomes peppered with mini-volcanoes in late spring courtesy of our ashy or grey mining bees (*Andrena cineraria*). Their silvery bodies, about the size of a slim honeybee, sparkle in the spring sunshine. The females are black with two broad, ashy-grey hairbands across the thorax. The males are similar, but the thorax is entirely clothed with less dense grey hairs, with a very pronounced tuft of white hairs on the lower face. Mating is energetic – pairs tumble across the grass in spring. So far I haven't managed to count them, but I'm told that females (like other Andrena species) have 12 segments to their antennae and the males 13. Looking at detail on live bees is a problem.

A male bee fly (*Bombylius major*)

The mining bees' nests are under attack – this one is being dive-bombed by a bumblebee

The ashy mining bee, one of the best pollinators of oilseed rape, is common in gardens, parks, calcareous grassland, orchards and on the edges of cropped agricultural land. We enjoy seeing these heaps of soil in the lawn, as do the blackbirds, who wait patiently and then pounce and carry off lots of ashy mining bees in their beaks for their hungry broods. The mining bees wriggle, although the blackbirds don't seem to notice.

If that were not devastating enough, bee-flies (*Bombyliidae*) also disrupt the ashy mining bees at Spring Cottage. These bee-like creatures, which are in fact flies, have straight proboscises that are permanently out. They love to visit cowslips and primulas, but will also visit muscari and other spring bulbs. When the time is ripe, they do a fly-past over the mining bees' holes and drop their eggs down into them. In order to aid their cause, the adult females of some species collect dust or sand at the tip of their abdomen, using it to coat their eggs and so provide camouflage and add extra weight. The bee-fly's larva hatches, crawls further into the bee's burrow and waits for the bee's own larva to grow to almost full size, at which point the bee-fly larva attacks the bee larva, feeding on its body fluids and eventually killing it. Year on year, however, we still have ashy mining bees, despite all the carnage.

Bumblebees also join in the destruction in some years, trying to force their bodies into fairly slender holes. When this occurs the ashy mining bees join

This leaf-cutter bee carries pollen on its under sides

forces and see off the intruder. I haven't seen this with bee-flies though.

I've also seen rusty mining bees (*A. fulva*) in fairly large numbers. They pollinate the gooseberries and early raspberries here, although we haven't knowingly seen their burrows. Andrenas are the largest bee genus in Britain and Ireland, with 67 species, so I'm sure we must have others. The females dig the nest, stock it with nectar and pollen and then seal it, leaving the young to fend for themselves.

LEAFCUTTER BEES

By early summer some of my roses will have had some circular discs removed from the foliage. This is the work of the leafcutter bee. Last year one made a nest in a pot of pelargoniums on the greenhouse bench, going in and out of the holes at the bottom, leaf in mouth. We had to leave the greenhouse door ajar so that work could carry on throughout the daylight hours. When the pot was moved outside, the work continued. These bees will also nest in old wooden posts and hollow plant stems. The leaves are rolled into a cigar shape and used to form 'cells' within the nest cavity. After finding a suitable spot (often near where she emerged), a female starts building a first cell, stocks it with a supply of food (pollen or a pollen/nectar mix) and oviposits (deposits an egg in it). She then builds a wall that separates the completed cell from the next one, plugging up the ends; several cells will be arranged close together. The larva hatches from the egg and consumes the food supply. After moulting a few times, it spins a cocoon and pupates.

The leafcutter bee we see is a species of *Megachile* and it resembles a honeybee in size and shape. There are seven species of leafcutter in the British Isles and Jennifer Owen recorded five of them, the most common being *Megachile willughbiella* or Willoughby's leafcutter bee. This is the most frequently seen species and very easy to identify because it carries its pollen underneath its body almost like a yellow rug. It adores the heleniums here, but is also known to like thistles, brambles and bellflowers. It uses bee hotels as well as pelargonium pots. Jeremy Early, writing

GOLDEN RULE

Tolerate some damage from leafcutter bees. They are highly efficient pollinators, so it's a lucky break.

in *My Side of the Fence*, used bee and bug hotels in his garden, positioning them by the greenhouse so that he could watch and photograph. His success has made me less sceptical about manufactured boxes, which I've always scorned in the past. In fact, one bee hotel positioned on the dry, east-facing wall of our summer house has been used and two of the dozen or so tubes have been capped.

HOVERFLIES

Once summer warms up you'll see lots of hoverflies in a variety of shapes and sizes. Numbers vary from year to year, and in my experience a warm summer encourages a lot more than a cool one. Many of those found in gardens are immigrants, so populations fluctuate according to the weather. There are approximately 285 species of hoverfly in Britain, and about half of these have larvae that prey on aphids and other small insects, so hoverflies can be very useful at controlling pests. They also pollinate flowers, but tend to select small flowers, or open flat flowers, because they have small mouth parts. Most look like small yellow-banded wasps, although there is no sting. Their ability to hover, almost standing still in mid-air, and their one pair of wings make them easy to spot.

Hoverflies seem to love yellow flowers. This one is getting nectar from *Achillea* 'Moonshine'

A white hoverfly egg on hardheads (*Centaurea nigra*)

Hoverfly larva on feverfew

Pupating hoverfly on the same feverfew plant

Hoverfly 'pooh'

The villain of the group is the large narcissus fly (*Merodon equestris*). This mimics a bumblebee, but it is a hoverfly despite that, and it drops its eggs on your prized bulbs. The larvae wriggle down and appear to feed on your bulbs and destroy them. In fact, they're feeding on microbes from rotting bulbs and not on healthy bulb tissue. The adults are busiest in warm weather in late spring and early summer and, should you have good enough hearing, you will hear a high-pitched whine. Those with sharp hearing race about with fly-swats, and one famous narcissus breeder, Alec Gray, once killed 300 flies in a few hours using one of these. I am not well blessed in the aural department and fret about my snowdrops every year. Many of them grow in open positions where the large narcissus fly prefers to operate. Gray advised 'swatting them between 10am and 4pm on sunny, warm days'.

> *The villain of the group is the large narcissus fly. This mimics a bumblebee, but it is a hoverfly and drops its eggs on your prized bulbs.*

Jennifer Owen's *Wildlife of a Garden* covers hoverflies very thoroughly, because this was the group of insects she was most interested in. She tells us that most garden hoverflies she found, and the majority of the most common species, have aphid-eating larvae, which is good news. She identified 94 species in her 30-year study and of these 57 were aphid-eaters. She noted that 81 per cent of all the individual hoverflies trapped consumed aphids and August was the month when she found most. It indicates how useful they are to the gardener.

Hoverflies are true flies and they follow the same lifecycle of adult, egg, larva and pupa. Like all true flies, the adults have just one pair of true wings. Behind each true wing is a small club-shaped structure known as a haltere. This acts like a gyroscope and gives these insects incredible control over their flight, allowing them to hover.

The adults visit flowers to find energy-giving nectar, or sometimes feed on honeydew. Females also collect and ingest protein-rich pollen needed for producing viable eggs. Nearly all hoverflies have specialised mouth parts, so are restricted to visiting simple flowers that offer easy access. They like orange and yellow flowers and umbellifers.

Adults live for a month or two months, depending on species. The females lay single eggs, rather like slim, off-white rugby balls, close to aphid colonies. After five days these hatch into larvae. A larva passes through three stages, or instars, and at the end of each stage sheds its skin so that it can increase in size. The first and second instars last only a few days, but the third and largest instar may be very long-lived and may even overwinter. The third-stage instars do most of the feeding, although the food requirements of species vary. Some feed on ants, some on bees and some on wasps. Others feed on rotting detritus in wet soil or water, while yet others are stem-borers, feeding on particular plants. About 40 per cent of the British species, some 110, are aphid-eating specialists that do a lot of good in the garden.

Hoverfly larvae are difficult to see. My first experience was when I noticed a jelly-like blob which looked more like a bird dropping than a living thing.

Hoverfly larvae are difficult to see. My first experience was when I noticed a jelly-like blob which looked more like a bird dropping than a living thing. It was completely stationary for the whole day, so I had a good look at it and realised that this one was a nocturnal hoverfly larva. Others do wriggle about in the day, rather like small milky slugs. They pupate, often close to pollen sources, and then a new hoverfly emerges. Although I have seen the pupae, I've never as yet seen one emerge.

The larva of *Episyrphus balteatus*, the marmalade hoverfly, eats hundreds of aphids during its development. It's mainly nocturnal, so stays hidden during the day. One larva is said to be able to consume between 250 and 600 cabbage aphids in its lifetime.

Another commonly found hoverfly, *Syrphus ribesii*, has extremely short mouth parts so feeds only on very open flowers. It will go from egg to adult within three weeks, and the first tiny instar will take 80 minutes to eat one aphid. The third instar will polish one off in four minutes. This overwinters as a larva and then pupates in the following spring. I often find the larvae on blackcurrant foliage when I'm picking.

Hoverflies are more effective at finding aphids than ladybirds, even though they are blind. They eat aphids more quickly and can reach into tighter spaces than ladybirds. Though there's still a lot to learn about them, it's obvious how useful most are in the garden.

LACEWINGS

I know that we have lacewings here, because they creep into the house during winter, usually staying close to a window. They make their homes in between the shed roof and the lining and once, when we had a gale that stripped away the black felt, we could see at least 100 lacewings exposed to the elements. There

Lacewing eggs suspended from a scabious flower

A lacewing larva devouring aphids

An adult *Chrysopherla carnea* – the common green lacewing

are 20 species of green lacewing in the UK and 29 species of brown lacewing. Jennifer Owen found 8 species of green lacewing and 9 species of brown lacewing in her garden.

The most familiar is the common green lacewing (*Chrysoperla carnea*). This is large (2–3 cm/1 in), with delicately veined, translucent wings. It has small, copper-brown eyes, lacy wings and a green body, which turns pinkish-brown in the autumn. The adults of *Chrysoperla carnea* feed only on honeydew and pollen, but their larvae feed on aphids and other small insects. Adult lacewings of other genera may be predatory.

Lacewing larvae are particularly voracious. I once read a Victorian gardening book that mentioned sending the garden boy out to collect 'lacewing lions' in his cap and bring them into the vinery to control an aphid attack. Spotting one for the first time was a triumph, and I watched as the ridged larva spent a long time eating aphids, tossing them up in the air, reminding me of a small seahorse. It seemed like one a minute! It's said that lacewing larvae frequently put the remains of their victims onto their own backs to act as camouflage, although I haven't seen this. I believe the number of trees on our cottage boundary draws the lacewings up into the foliar canopy, so I rarely see many on herbaceous plants. I sometimes find the empty cases of lacewing larvae in April or May, indicating that they've just emerged. Their empty shells often glint in the sunlight after an April shower.

I watched as the ridged larva spent a long time eating aphids, tossing them up in the air, reminding me of a small seahorse.

These insects are so good at hunting aphids that they are reared for biological pest control. The female green lacewings lay eggs in batches on stalks, sticking them on with a drop of gummy fluid. We've seen them suspended from scabious flowers, like swings on a carousel.

BUTTERFLIES

Butterflies add a touch of magic to the garden and I am always excited to see the first red admiral or peacock emerging from hibernation, battered and fading though it might be. We have seen 22 species of butterfly here between March and the end of September. However, the weather plays an enormous part and there are far more in sunny, warm summers than in cool, damp affairs.

Most gardens will have enough butterfly-friendly flowers for common butterflies, but to attract rarer species you have to consider both the habitat and the food plants the caterpillars need, because butterflies are very specific feeders.

Buddleja davidii is a magnet for butterflies, and planted in a warm position its flowers will attract 20 species, according to Butterfly Conservation. The key is to provide shelter and warmth so that the nectar flows. On one August day we counted 84 freshly emerged peacocks on our buddleia bush.

THE BROWNS (SATYRIDAE)

In recent years the long areas of flower-studded grass in the mini-meadow and on the road verges have increased the number of Brown butterflies. They roost in long grass and also use grasses to lay their eggs on, and we have seen female ringlets flying very low over the mini-meadow, laying eggs as they go. Some of the commoner Browns lay on coarse grasses, even couch grass (*Elytrigia repens*), but others prefer finer fescues. In all, 17 of our resident butterfly species feed on grasses or sedges, and 11 of these are brown butterflies, of which we have seen six. When it comes to food plants (i.e. grasses), the full range is not generally known.

> ## GOLDEN RULE
> --------------------------
> **Plant at least one buddleia in a sunny position.**

Speckled wood (*Pararge aegeria*)
This dark butterfly with yellow spots is seen here every year between March and late October, almost always in shady spots. However, it's most noticeable in autumn, feeding on asters in the autumn border. For most of the year speckled woods feed on honeydew in the tree tops, but when aphid activity declines they turn their attention to flowers. Eggs are laid on coarser grasses, including couch grass – and yes, we do have some!

Food plants: False brome (*Brachypodium sylvaticum*), Cock's-foot (*Dactylis glomerata*), Yorkshire fog (*Holcus lanatus*), Common couch (*Elytrigia repens*)

The circles on the underwing explain the name of the ringlet

The small heath butterfly on a salad burnet

Gatekeeper (*Pyronia tithonus*)

This orange and brown butterfly has a black eyespot on the forewing containing two white dots. Although similar to the meadow brown, it is brighter in colour. It's very keen on marjoram and adores *Origanum laevigatum* 'Herrenhausen', although it usually appears here in early July before these flower. The eggs are laid mostly on finer grasses.

Food plants: Bents (*Agrostis* species), Fescues (*Festuca* species), Meadow-grasses (*Poa* species), Common couch (*Elytrigia repens*)

Meadow brown (*Maniola jurtina*)

Just as common as the gatekeeper here, this is a larger butterfly with duller brown markings and it appears before the gatekeeper, usually in June. The eyespots have single white pupils. Prefers finer grasses, but will use coarse grasses if need be.

Food plants: Fescues (*Festuca* species), Bents (*Agrostis* species), Meadow grasses (*Poa* species), Cock's-foot (*Dactylis glomerata*), Downy oat-grass (*Helictotrichon pubescens*), False brome (*Brachypodium sylvaticum*)

Ringlet (*Aphantopus hyperantus*)

Freshly hatched in late June or early July, this butterfly resembles sooty-black velvet edged in pale cream – rather like Guinness in a glass. They roost with their wings closed, displaying the small circles on their under-wing that earn them the name of ringlet. Lots of them roost (and hopefully lay eggs) on the verges closest to the spring.

Food plants: Cock's-foot (*Dactylis glomerata*), False brome (*Brachypodium sylvaticum*), Tufted hair grass (*Deschampsia cespitosa*), Common couch (*Elytrigia repens*), Meadow grasses (*Poa* species)

Gatekeeper butterfly on marjoram

Small heath (*Coenonympha pamphilus*)
A much smaller butterfly, normally seen resting with its wings closed. It's often earlier, from May onwards here, but we do not see that many compared to other Brown species. They're known to be territorial, so males can be seen fighting together, and they tend to stay in the same areas year on year. Likes low-growing flowers, such as thyme, and lays eggs on finer grasses.

Food plants: Fescues (*Festuca* species), Meadow grasses (*Poa* species), Bents (*Agrostis* species)

Marbled white (*Melanargia galathea*)
This black-and-white chequered butterfly is a brown, despite its markings. It occasionally drifts through the garden in midsummer, more so since the wildflower strips along the fields were created. It is often seen on wild orchids, but here it usually settles on knapweed flowers (*Centaurea nigra*), although it's almost certainly passing through. Red fescue is an essential part of the diet of the larvae. Once found only on limestone grassland in southern England, the range is extending northwards and eastwards.

Food plants: Red fescue (*Festuca rubra*), Sheep's fescue (*F. ovina*), Yorkshire fog (*Holcus lanatus*), Tor-grass (*Brachypodium pinnatum*)

MOTH-LIKE BUTTERFLIES (HESPERIIDAE)

To many people, skippers look more like moths, with their upper wings appearing to be held above their lower wings. They like rough, grassy tussocks, in which they hide, so this makes them hard to see. However, when they do fly they seem to skip above the grass, hence their name. They are tricky to identify when basking and too fast in flight for us, although they fly only in sunlight. They do loop the loops. We know we have the large and the small skipper, and see them both in high summer.

Large skipper (*Ochlodes sylvanus*)
A sturdy skipper with long antennae clubbed at the end. The males have orange upper wings margined in brown with a few pale-orange spots. Males have a thick black line through the centre of the forewing, and their wings appear to

look chequered. The undersides have faint orange spots, unlike the bright silver spots of the silver-spotted skipper.

Food plants: Cock's-foot (*Dactylis glomerata*) – preferred plant, Purple moor grass (*Molinia caerulea*), False brome (*Brachypodium sylvaticum*), Tor-grass (*B. pinnatum*), Wood small-reed (*Calamagrostis epigejos*)

Small skipper (*Thymelicus sylvestris*)

Only slightly smaller than the large skipper, this butterfly has vivid orange-brown wings held with forewings angled above the hind wings. Males have a thin black line through the centre of the forewing.

Food plants: Yorkshire fog (*Holcus lanatus*) – preferred plant, Timothy grass (*Phleum pratense*), Creeping soft-grass (*Holcus mollis*), False brome (*Brachypodium sylvaticum*), Meadow foxtail (*Alopecurus pratensis*), Cock's-foot (*Dactylis glomerata*)

THE WHITES (PIERIDAE)

This family contains some villains and some charmers. Let's start with the charmers.

THE CHARMING WHITES

Brimstone (*Gonepteryx rhamni*)

This is the butterfly seen in spring, quite often just as the wild bluebells open, and there is a view, according to Butterfly Conservation, that the word 'butterfly' actually describes the acid-yellow colour of the male. The females are more clotted-cream. Although it can be seen in any month, the two peaks are in spring and in high summer, and the weather has to be warm and sunny. It adores pink and purple flowers, and favourites here are buddleia and the everlasting pea (*Lathyrus latifolius*). Their very long tongues help them greatly.

Food plants: Buckthorn (*Rhamnus cathartica*), Alder buckthorn (*Frangula alnus*)

Orange tip (*Anthocharis cardamines*)

Easily recognised, because the male of this small white butterfly has orange tips to its wings. The females have dark black tips instead. Both have mottled-green under-wings, but mostly these butterflies are recognisable because they move very swiftly. Birds and other predators ignore them because their bodies are full of mustard oil from the brassicas the caterpillars consumed. As the species name suggests, their preferred larval plant is the cuckooflower (*Cardamine pratensis*), so they emerge in April once this plant is almost flowering. There are many other Brassica-family plants that also support the larvae, and we have seen the slim

Orange tip butterflies are often about on a warm April day. These were mating

green caterpillars on Jack-by-the-hedge or garlic mustard (*Alliaria petiolata*). It will also lay eggs on honesty (*Lunaria annua*) and sweet rocket (*Hesperis matronalis*), but with less success.

Food plants: Cuckooflower (*Cardamine pratensis*), Garlic mustard (*Alliaria petiolata*), Hedge mustard (*Sisymbrium officinale*), Winter-cress (*Barbarea vulgaris*)

Green-veined white (*Pieris napi*)

A small, white butterfly with green veining on the underside of the wing. It likes moist places and the spring at the bottom of the garden may lure it in. It's delicate in looks and flight, the males fluttering through in mid-April and then in high summer. Females lie low, close to plants, looking for a wild Brassica host, although not cultivated brassica crops.

Food plants: Garlic mustard (*Alliaria petiolata*), Cuckooflower (*Cardamine pratensis*), Hedge mustard (*Sisymbrium officinale*), Watercress (*Rorippa nasturtium-aquaticum*), Charlock (*Sinapis arvensis*), Large bittercress (*Cardamine amara*), Wild cabbage (*Brassica oleracea*), Wild radish (*Raphanus raphanistrum*)

THE VILLAINOUS WHITES

Large white (*Pieris brassicae*)

Most commonly called the cabbage white, because this large, strong butterfly lays clusters of eggs on your cabbage plants and then eats them down to the stalks. The brilliant-white wings have black tips on the forewings, extending down to the wing edge. Females also have two black spots on their forewings not present in males. Undersides are creamy-white with two spots. The increase in fields of oilseed rape has made them more of a problem. One predatory wasp, *Cotesia glomerata*, lays eggs in the emerging caterpillars and the sulphur-yellow cocoons rupture the caterpillar's yellow-and-black body (see page 153).

This large, strong butterfly lays clusters of eggs on your cabbage plants and then eats them down to the stalks.

Food plants: All members of the Brassica family, including commercial crops such as oilseed rape, cultivated Brassicas, Nasturtium (*Tropaeolum majus*), Sea stock (*Matthiola incana*), sweet rocket (*Hesperis matronalis*)

Small white (*Pieris rapae*)

Just a smaller version of the large white, it lays single eggs on your cultivated Brassicas. The lone green caterpillar then heads straight into the middle of a cabbage where it does rather a lot of damage. August is generally the worst month, and butterfly netting is the only solution. Keep it there all year, for as the caterpillars disappear the pigeons take over.

Food plants: Cultivated Brassicas, Nasturtium (*Tropaeolum majus*), Sea stock (*Matthiola incana*), sweet rocket (*Hesperis matronalis*)

THE BLUES (LYCAENIDAE)

Small, colourful butterflies (not all of them blue), often with wings that gleam, these can be encouraged by planting wildflowers in your meadow areas. Most prefer unfertilised grassland, but we see the following every year in the garden, often feeding on low-growing thymes and dwarf marjoram.

Common blue (*Polyommatus icarus*)

This is our commonest grassland blue butterfly, on the wing during May and June and then again in mid-September. The upper wings are a bright blue and the undersides display lots of orange, while the uppers have a pure-white uninterrupted margin. The caterpillars use legumes as food plants and may have a casual association with ants. The chrysalis does have a relationship with ants and can be found in the nests of red ants (*Myrmica sabulati*).

Food plants: Common bird's-foot-trefoil (*Lotus corniculatus*), Greater bird's-foot-trefoil (*L. pedunculatus*), Black medick (*Medicago lupulina*), Common restharrow (*Ononis repens*), White clover (*Trifolium repens*), Lesser trefoil (*T. dubium*)

Often described as hyperactive, their pristine orange-and-brown wings are a priceless sight.

Small copper (*Lycaena phlaeas*)

Probably my favourite butterfly, because it feeds on thyme plants growing in the paving at the front of the house. Although numbers vary from year to year, we're helped by the amount of larvae-feeding sorrel growing in the fields nearby and, when the weather's kind, we can have five small coppers on one thyme plant. We presume that these are females, which are similar to the males only larger. Male small coppers are notoriously territorial, but no fights break out. Often described as hyperactive, their pristine orange-and-brown wings are a priceless sight. I have tried growing sorrel in the garden, but found it was too invasive, self-seeding far too freely.

Common blues like eryngiums. They occasionally roost in our long grass too

Food plants: Common sorrel (*Rumex acetosa*), Sheep's sorrel (*R. acetosella)*, Broad-leaved dock (*R. obtusifolius*) – just occasionally

Brown argus (*Aricia agestis*)

Although brown in colour, this small, dark butterfly still belongs to the Blues. It pops up now and again in a good summer in a garden hotspot, although you may never see it because it's found mainly on southern chalk and limestone grassland. When the wings are open they display an orange 'necklace' border. Here it feeds on simply shaped pinks (dianthus). We have rock-roses, *Geranium pyrenaicum*, *G. pratense* and erodiums in the garden, which may attract egg-laying females, although we have never seen any eggs or caterpillars inthe garden.

Food plants: Common rock-rose (*Helianthemum nummularium*), Dove's-foot crane's-bill (*Geranium molle*), Common stork's-bill (*Erodium cicutarium*), Cut-leaved crane's-bill (*G. dissectum*), Meadow crane's-bill (*G. pratense*), Hedgerow crane's-bill (*G. pyrenaicum*)

Holly blue (*Celastrina argiolus*)

You should see this small blue butterfly in your garden in early spring, because it's the commonest blue butterfly in gardens. It's very similar to the common blue, but the undersides of the holly blue are pale blue with small black spots. The common blue has orange marks on the under-wing and an undisturbed white rim. Spring generations feed on holly, but the summer generations feed on ivy. A dead pigeon, hidden in a border, unbeknown to me, attracted several holly blues, and I have seen blues feeding on damp dung in fields nearby.

> *A dead pigeon hidden in a border attracted several holly blues, and I have seen blues feeding on damp dung in fields nearby.*

Food plants: Holly (*Ilex aquifolium*) for the spring generation, Ivy (*Hedera helix*) for the summer generation, Spindle (*Euonymus europaeus*), Dogwood (*Cornus* spp.), Snowberries (*Symphoricarpos* species), Gorses (*Ulex* species), Bramble (*Rubus fruticosus*)

NETTLE-RELATED BUTTERFLIES

The stinging nettle is a plant gardeners tend to shun, but if you have a clump of nettles in a sunny position you could entice five species of butterflies to lay their eggs – the peacock, red admiral, small tortoiseshell, comma and occasionally painted lady.

Peacock (*Aglais io*)

With a name that sounds like a Greek taverna, this butterfly with the large eye spots is one of the commonest garden visitors. You see shabby specimens early on, ones that have overwintered in a crevice or shed, and I have even seen these on snowdrops. They are strong fliers and early-flowering males travel over half a mile in search of a good territory and a mate. Its preferred habitat is in the shelter of woodland clearings, rides and edges. Once they've mated, the female lays between 300 and 500 sticky green eggs on the top of the stinging nettle where the leaves are most nutritious. On hatching, the caterpillars spin a web and develop beneath the misty silk. These clusters are easily spotted, their dark-black, white-speckled bodies writhing together in a mass and then wandering away to pupate. To see a newly hatched peacock, all pristine, is a treat and there are often many of them about at the same time. They adore buddleias but also feed on many other garden flowers.

Food plants: Common nettle (*Urtica dioica*), Small nettle (*U. urens*) – occasionally Hop (*Humulus lupulus*)

Five small tortoiseshell butterflies feeding on buddleia

Small tortoiseshell (*Aglais urticae*)

Another common butterfly, with orange-and-black wings decorated with a blue-and-black edging. It's seen in spring, but is most common in August when it feeds on origanums, buddleia and asters. It had a population dip in the 1990s but seems to have recovered. We often see clusters of three, four or five squabbling, or displaying in August. Like the peacock, it has caterpillars that feed on nettles, under a similar silk screen. However, these caterpillars have yellow on their bodies.

Food plants: Common nettle (*Urtica dioica*), Small nettle (*U. urens*)

Red admiral (*Vanessa atalanta*)

This strong-flying butterfly, which is the only black, red and white butterfly, overwinters and is often the first butterfly of the year because it flies in low temperatures. However, numbers are boosted by migrants from North Africa and continental Europe. The immigrant females lay eggs and consequently there is an emergence of fresh butterflies from about July onwards. They continue flying into October or November. They love rotting fruit such as plums and apples, and also ivy flowers. They also adore buddleia and echinaceas. The eggs are laid singly, so this butterfly is not so fussy about a sunny site. There are more adults in warm summers here.

Food plants: Common nettle (*Urtica dioica*), Small nettle (*U. urens*), Pellitory-of-the-wall (*Parietaria judaica*), Hop (*Humulus lupulus*)

Painted lady (*Vanessa cardui*)

If there's a good summer we often see painted ladies speeding through the garden. Many arrive as migrants, spreading northwards from the desert fringes of North Africa, the Middle East and Central Asia. They recolonise mainland Europe before reaching Britain and Ireland in May or June. Their offspring are most noticeable in the second half of summer and in some years you see lots, in others none.

Food plants: Thistles (*Cirsium* species and *Carduus* species), Mallows (*Malva* species), Common nettle (*Urtica dioica*) – occasionally, Viper's-bugloss (*Echium vulgare*)

Comma (*Polygonia c-album*)

This orange-and-brown butterfly has a distinctively shaped lower wing resembling a comma. The rest of the wings have a scalloped edge, and this broken outline and the tawny colour allows the adults to hide and hibernate among the foliage. Caterpillars resemble bird droppings, another camouflage. We see adults often at Spring Cottage and, although it has been in decline, it seems to thrive in our area and is coming back in others. We have seen this caterpillar feeding on gooseberry bushes and it's thought that a new strain of comma, possibly of European origin, uses different food plants. The older strain fed mostly on hops.

Food plants: Common nettle (*Urtica dioica*), Hop (*Humulus lupulus*), Elm (*Ulmus* species), Currants (*Ribes* species), Willows (*Salix* species)

ALSO FOUND AT SPRING COTTAGE

Silver-washed fritillary (*Argynnis paphia*)

A high-flying, very large butterfly that sometimes skims through the garden in August. The pointed wings and silver streaks on the undersides separate it from other fritillaries.

Food plants: Common dog-violet (*Viola riviniana*)

BIRDLIFE

Spring Cottage is not a wonderful garden for birds. We seem to be at the wrong end of the village. The church end, with its mature gardens planted up decades ago, graveyard and allotments is far better than our end. In winter when the weather's cold the bird feeders attract the usual suspects. Greenfinches, coal tits, long-tailed tits, blue tits and occasionally nuthatches and blackcaps visit the nuts and sunflower seeds. The spotted woodpecker also likes the peanuts. However, in mild winters the feeders can stay full for days because the birds, who tend to travel in flocks, have moved elsewhere. It's worth putting peanuts out in summer for your woodpeckers, for the adults are very grateful when they're feeding fledglings. Later in the year, you may be rewarded by family groups in various stages of plumage.

Feeding birds is very worthy and I highly recommend it. Looking at birds over breakfast is much better than watching daytime television.

Feeding birds is very worthy and I highly recommend it. Looking at birds over breakfast is much better than watching daytime television. However, it doesn't generally help the next generation, because most baby birds in their nests need small invertebrates, such as grubs, flies, aphids and worms. Seeds simply won't do for most. I have already said that blue tits need to gather 10,000 invertebrates in three weeks to feed the average brood. Mature trees provide lots of food, particularly oaks, as did the 50-year-old cooking-apple tree in my old garden in Hook Norton, which saw blue tits toing and froing in the nesting season. These birds will be frisking your garden and removing many of the creatures you deem to be pests. It's another good reason to run a chemical-free garden.

OUR PERMANENT STAFF

Birds travel – that's why they have wings – so the blackbird we see again and again is almost certainly not the same one. They visit several gardens within a territory and we can count on the following to be in the garden most days, although the likelihood is they'll be different birds working an area. Birds also moult and, minus their feathers, they lie low so may go AWOL for a week or two. We notice these quiet weeks.

Wren (*Troglodytes troglodytes*)
We always see plenty of wrens in the garden and we hear their chit-chit-chittering alarm call, especially in spring. They're tiny, a rich brown, and they flit about with their tails cocked up in the air. They frisk the autumn border

looking for insects, they scour the netting over the brassicas and nip underneath if there's a gap to get at whitefly and aphids. They'll enter the shed, the greenhouse and cold frames, fearlessly darting in and out, although wrens are always furtive and rather secretive. They also take lots of spiders. However, they are knocked back by hard winters due to their size and their specialised diet of insects and larvae. This is difficult to replicate on a bird table. They don't migrate, so tend to get clobbered by cold winters. We used to have a patch of brambles over the wall and when this was cleared our wrens disappeared for a couple of years. Cover is important to them.

Wrens use lots of fallen leaves and moss to produce their nests

An estimated 5 million pairs breed in Britain. It's said that you should never move a wren's nest, a woven concoction made of moss, leaves and grass, because the males build them for the females, who then line them with feathers when they decide they need them. Ours almost certainly nest in two places – in the wild area behind the cottage and in the arborescent ivy growing into the whitebeam tree by the spring. Pigeons also nest there, so the ivy is a mixed blessing.

Blackbird (*Turdus merula*)

We see blackbirds every day and mostly the males are soot-black with bright-yellow beaks. However, in winter we get greyer blackbirds that are a different, slightly more upright shape with duller beaks, and these are migrant birds from the Continent. The BTO reports that hordes of blackbirds from Norway, Sweden and as far east as Finland come to spend the winter with us from autumn onwards. The females are a rich brown.

Blackbirds love fruit. When berries are about in autumn, they eat masses of them.

Blackbirds love fruit. When berries are about in autumn, they eat masses of them, beginning with cotoneaster, and they also love fallen apples. However, we have to grow our raspberries, currants and blueberries under netting, well away from their hungry beaks. It's also fascinating to watch them tugging worms from the lawn, or scooping up the mining bees.

For all that, I love them and their song, which, like that of many birds, is magnificent around mid-February when they are attracting a mate. They also have local dialects. The Hook Norton blackbirds used to say 'get out of it, get out

Robin

GOLDEN RULE

Feed your birds with sunflower seeds, peanuts and fat balls by all means, but remember that breeding birds almost always need invertebrates.

of it' repeatedly. The Gloucestershire blackbirds have an entirely different intonation, a bit like the Best Beloved's soft burr. They are also the most amazing mothers, feeding birds almost as large as themselves and giving them flying lessons.

Robin (*Erythacus rubecula*)

Gardeners love robins. They are the bird that gets almost close enough for you to touch if you're digging or weeding. As soon as you move, they're on the patch of soil looking for slug eggs or grubs. You don't have to wait until spring to hear their high-pitched song, either. They are so territorial they sing throughout winter as well, although not nearly as melodically as when spring arrives. In full breeding mode their musical song sounds almost flute-like, and they show themselves off as they sing, rather like Teddy boys at dances – spruced and looking for trouble.

Robins can be very aggressive and I have witnessed some battles here, presumably between two males. They eat berries, and the spindle tree (*Euonymus alatus*) is a favourite. If a robin finds a good bush, he will protect it from others and fight to the death to do so; 10 per cent of older robins die defending their territory.

The name 'robin' is relatively modern: before the 15th century the bird was commonly known just as the redbreast, but also as the ruddock or robinet, from which today's name derives. They are associated with Christmas cards because these used to be delivered by the red-coated postmen who were nicknamed robins.

Woodpigeon (*Columba palumbus*)

A clumsy Latin name for a clumsy-footed, big-breasted bird – quite like a description of me in fact (*Bournus rotunda*). It does one good job for me. It eats lots of seeds from the beech masts and so, hopefully, prevents lots of seedlings sprouting up. And it coos in summer, catching the softness of the season. The wood pigeon is large and blue-grey in colour, with a shimmering pink chest and a white neck patch when adult. On days when there's a shoot, hundreds take to the air, but we seem to have our resident Howard and Hilda either nesting in the ivy of the whitebeam or in the large trees nearby. They are also good mothers, feeding their babies with milk formed from sloughing off fluid-filled cells in the crop lining. This is more nutritious than human or cow's milk.

THE BIRD-SEED BRIGADE

These birds come looking for food in the feeders and some, like the chaffinch, are ground-feeders, picking up the crumbs from the table. Most are travelling through in winter, although we do have nesting pairs of goldfinches, blue tits, coal tits and great tits either in the garden or very close by. The great tits sometimes use the bird boxes on the side of the summer house.

> *Bird feeders are popular locations for birds of prey and the sparrowhawk reduces the numbers of these smaller birds.*

Bird feeders are popular locations for birds of prey, and the sparrowhawk (*Accipiter nisus*), which is around in the village, reduces the numbers of these smaller birds every year by swooping down on feeding stations. We haven't seen it near our feeders, but they are positioned close to the house and this may be a deterrent. At Hook Norton the resident sparrow population was reduced by one a day when the hobby (*Falco subbuteo*), a summer visitor, swooped in. You could almost set the clock by it, as it struck around midday, coming down like a sparrow-eating swift in an arc, in the blink of an eye. The sparrows would go quiet when it was about.

Chaffinch (*Fringilla coelebs*)

Very useful at frisking my gooseberries and removing any sawfly larvae, this pink-toned, sparrow-sized finch has a slate-blue crown and two white wing bars. They are so diligent, preferring small caterpillars, and for this reason they nest late, in late-April or May.

A pair of bluetits on a winter's day

Greenfinch (*Carduelis chloris*)

A greenish-yellow, sparrow-sized bird that feeds on a variety of seeds, including peanuts and sunflower seeds, but preferring black sunflower. A few can empty a feeder in three hours or so. They tend to stay put and monopolise the feeders in really cold conditions.

Coal tit (*Periparus ater*)

A darty little bird, smaller than the blue tit, with pinkish colouring and a black cap separated by a white Mohican stripe. It's the fastest feeder of all, nipping in and out, fearlessly, and taking the seed away in its beak. It can be displaced by larger birds. Although found in gardens, coal tits have an affinity for conifers, as do greenfinches, and their slender bill allows them to collect conifer seeds. Coal tits begin nesting slightly earlier than blue tits and some time before great tits.

Blue tit (*Cyanistes caeruleus*)

Ubiquitous in gardens, this jaunty, acrobatic little bird has a dark blue-black eye-stripe and a brighter blue 'skullcap' set against white cheeks and forehead, contrasting with a lemon-yellow chest. Bird ringers have proved that many dozens of blue tits can pass through a garden on a single day. They pick over the foliage on our young apple and pear trees, planted about eight years ago, and also frisk the roses.

Great tit (*Parus major*)

Similar in colour to the blue tit, but larger and with a domed black head and a black vertical stripe down the middle of its yellow underside. The call is a robust 'teacher-teacher'. They nest in or very near the garden, probably because of the beech trees round Spring Cottage. For much of the year they eat the seeds from the trees, but do not forage on the ground for them as the pigeons do.

Long-tailed tit (*Aegithalos caudatus*)

This looks more like a cotton-wool ball with a black tail than a bird, but you rarely see one on its own. They travel *en masse* and roost *en masse*, averaging between 8 and 20 in each flock. They prefer fat balls, which we don't put out because they attract rats. They've benefited from supplementary feeding in the last few years across the country. Here they go to the peanuts and nibble them.

Long-tailed tits begin breeding earlier in the year than other tits. They may start to construct an elaborate domed nest in late February in southern England. The nests are often placed high up in the fork of a tree, or lower down in a thorny shrub such as hawthorn. The nest is made of moss, woven together with spider webs and hair, camouflaged on the outside with lichens and lined with an average of 1,500 feathers.

Nuthatch (*Sitta europaea*)

You cannot mistake this bird on a feeder, because it's nearly always upside down with its head at the bottom. The back is a steel-grey and the underside a buff-pink, but the giveaways are the dramatic black eye stripe and short dagger-like bill. We do not see

A great tit with a beak full of wriggling things

them that often, which is strange, because they are said to be very sedentary – moving only from tree to tree. I once taught at a school and saw them on my way in at eight in the morning on most days. They nest in large mature trees, especially conifers. So if you find yourself grubbing out an old *Leylandii* hedge, leave one or two in situ as a refuge.

Nuthatches go for peanuts and are known to carry them off and bury them, rather like jays. They also place nuts, including peanuts, in crevices and hammer them with their bills.

Great spotted woodpecker (*Dendrocopos major*)

This starling-sized bird is black and white with red underneath the tail. Adult males also have a red nape. They do need woodland nearby, because they eat beetle larvae and grubs from dead and decaying wood. Our wooden sculptures have been ravaged and we can hear the repetitive drilling quite often. There's a shock-absorber system between the bird's beak and skull, so any stresses are transmitted directly towards the centre of the brain. When woodpeckers hammer into wood to get at grubs they make use of very long tongues which protrude 4 cm (1½ in) beyond the beak, so they can harpoon insect larvae

There's a shock–absorber system between the bird's beak and skull, so any stresses are transmitted directly towards the centre of the brain.

A young green woodpecker being trained up by an adult on our lawn

in their long tunnels. Here we see them on peanuts, which they like to carry away, if the feeder allows them, to an old line post. They cram the nuts in the top, using it like a vice, and then consume the nuts away from the feeder.

Goldfinch (*Carduelis carduelis*)

These small finches are very brightly coloured, with black and red on the head and yellow wing stripes. You often hear them before you see them as they make a constant 'tswitt-witt-witt'. Goldfinches mass together in small flocks during winter, often mixed up with other finches and tits. However, we see them throughout the year and the one plant they really adore is the teasel (*Dipsacus fullonum*). I grow it on the edges especially for them, but have to remove seedlings from vegetable beds and borders. They also adore thistles.

In sun goldfinches gleam and sparkle and regularly frisk the borders for seeds and insects.

LESS OBVIOUS VISITORS

It makes me enormously sad that birds I once thought two-a-penny only 30 years ago are now in much shorter supply. We do still see garrulous house sparrows (*Passer domesticus*), but not nearly as many. In the late 1960s every garden had a flock. The BTO completed a survey and concluded that house sparrows occur with higher frequency where sites are close to farmland than they do where they are close to suburban features such as schools, parks or wasteground. Loft insulation in houses has also been a factor in driving them out: they can't squeeze into roofs like they used to. If you have them, enjoy them and encourage them.

The song thrush (*Turdus philomelos*), with its melodic thrice-repeated song, is another in decline, leading to it being red-listed as a bird of serious conservation concern. Long-term monitoring carried out by the BTO showed that the population in England fell by more than 50 per cent between 1970 and 1995, although there has been a partial recovery during the last decade.

The decline was most pronounced on farmland, where the population decreased by about 70 per cent. The fall in numbers has probably been caused by the loss and degradation of preferred feeding and nesting habitats such as hedgerows and wet ditches. The thrush needs damp soil to find food in. There's far less grazed permanent pasture (especially cow pastures) now than in the past, and woodland patches on farms, important habitats with plenty of food for song thrushes, are often removed. The RSPB has compared populations on intensively farmed arable land with mixed farmland. Two major differences were found. Thrushes on intensively farmed arable land made only two or three nesting attempts each year and a few of their fledglings appeared to survive their first few weeks after leaving the nest. Thrushes on mixed farms attempted to nest four or five times and had a better success rate.

Although the thrush's decline is largely caused by factors outside the control of gardeners, it may well be that naturally run gardens could be really important for their survival.

The starling (*Sturnus vulgaris*) is in the same boat, vanishing before our eyes. Their black bodies, iridescent in the sun, and spangled in green and gold somehow don't quite compensate for what is a rather dishevelled bird. So numerous as to be a pest right up until the early 1990s, it has now declined. There are winter migrants of course, murmurating acrobatically over some estuary or other, but few residents in summer.

Red kites, once very rare, are now often seen reeling over our garden

The BTO tells us that the number of breeding starlings in the UK has fallen rapidly, particularly since the early 1980s.

The BTO tells us that the number of breeding starlings in the UK has fallen rapidly, particularly since the early 1980s, and especially in woodland. The declines have been greatest in the south and west of Britain, but recent Breeding Bird Survey (BBS) data suggest that populations are also decreasing in Scotland and Northern Ireland, where the trends were initially upward. The species has been upgraded from amber to red as the decline has become more severe. Strong improvements have occurred in breeding performance, but young birds fail to survive – almost certainly due to lack of food.

The starling was, of course, a fantastic pest controller. The website www.starlingtalk.com explains that more than half (57 per cent) of the annual food of the adult starling consists of animal matter, including insects, millipedes, spiders, molluscs, a few crustaceans, and bits of suet and carrion. In April and May such food constitutes more than 90 per cent of the bird's diet, and even in February, when the opportunities for obtaining animal food are few, it forms more than 28 per cent of the total. Nearly 75 per cent of the animal food of the starlings, or more than 42 per cent of its entire diet, consists of insects. October is the month of greatest consumption of insects, when they form nearly 58 per cent of food, but in June, August, September and November insects also provide more than half of the starling's sustenance.

NOT ALL GLOOM AND DOOM

It isn't all gloom and doom. For instance, we regularly see red kites here. I can remember travelling to Radnorshire in the early 1970s to see one of the few breeding pairs. I think there were 20 left in the 1960s, so I never thought one would fly over my garden, but now I see them quite regularly – sometimes squabbling with ravens, buzzards and jackdaws, all of whom come within spitting distance of the cottage. They mainly eat carrion and worms, but are opportunistic and will occasionally take small mammals. According to research carried out by Professor Mark Fellowes at Reading University's School of Biological Sciences, in 2015 there were believed to be 2,700 breeding pairs in Britain. Revivals can and do happen!

The hedgehog is one creature gardeners could help save from extinction

THE
GROUND
FORCE

-11-
THE GROUND FORCE

I've learnt that a lot of the living jigsaw happens either at ground level or below the ground, often at night. It's hard to observe, but just as important as the flying squad. Many of these 'on the ground' insects and small mammals play a role as predators. They need cover during daylight in order to survive in both your garden and mine. The most loved is certainly the hedgehog and this snuffling 'hedge pig' is happiest in gardens or close to them. It's in great decline and this is one creature that may well be saved from extinction by the actions of sympathetic gardeners.

HEDGEHOGS

Everyone loves the hedgehog, despite its prickles, but it's in a perilous situation. In 1950 – incidentally, the year of my birth – there were an estimated 36 million hedgehogs in the UK. By 2015 the numbers had plummeted to a mere million, which could mean that the hedgehog, once so ubiquitous, may be on the way to extinction within my lifetime, or my children's. Dr Pat Morris, who has studied hedgehogs for 50 years as man and boy, believes that gardens may become their last refuge, for urban populations have declined by one third since 2000, compared to their country cousins, who have gone down by half.

The hedgehog, once so ubiquitous, may be on the way to extinction within my lifetime.

Their greater rural decline has prompted some research by Dr Richard Yarnell on the Brackenhurst Campus, a rural outpost of Nottingham Trent University. He radio-tracked ten hedgehogs to find out more, and discovered that the 'Brackenhurst Ten' avoided arable land where food and protective cover would be much scarcer. The Ten also avoided badger setts – quite wisely, because badgers are their main predator. They also share the same insectivorous diet. Badger numbers are thought to have

doubled in recent years, so hedgehogs may struggle to find food in areas where there are many badgers.

Yarnell's 'Brackenhurst Ten' had circular routes and stuck close to hedgerows, by and large, walking along them. They also crossed pastureland which would contain dung-rich short turf. Pastures have far more earthworms than ploughed land and earthworms are their third most preferred food, after beetles and caterpillars. Traditional farming, which relied on smaller fields bounded by hedges, was hedgehog-friendly because many of these smaller fields would have been grazed by livestock and would have supported large numbers of insects including dung beetles. Dense hedges with wide bottoms have proved the most hedgehog-friendly of all. So edge habitats are important to them.

More than 122,000 hectares (more than 300,000 acres) of grassland have vanished in England since 1992.

Pastureland has disappeared in the countryside, even in recent times. More than 122,000 hectares (more than 300,000 acres) of grassland have vanished in England since 1992 according to the Campaign to Protect Rural England (CPRE) report, *Meadow Madness*. That's a slice of land equal to the county of Bedfordshire. Large arable fields, bounded by fences rather than hedges, are

Gardens may be the last refuge for these well-loved creatures

now the norm and they are definitely counterproductive to hedgehogs. So a major part of their decline must be that modern farming practices have worked against them. It's no wonder they've voted with their feet.

A study by Carly Pettett, an Oxford PhD student, involved 12 hedgehogs sourced from a rescue centre. She released them in spring on four diverse farms in rural Oxfordshire. Radio-tracking showed that ten headed straight off to nearby villages and gardens. It may be that they had been rescued in a garden setting and so returned to what they knew pre-rescue; or perhaps they associated food and shelter, and fewer badgers, with gardens surrounding houses.

Dr Yarnell's Nottinghamshire study may have the answer to why ten of the 'Oxfordshire Dozen' voted with their feet. He found that when it came to building nests, whether for day use or hibernation, his 'Brackenhurst Ten' stayed close to the buildings on the campus: 31 hibernation nests found were in brambles, hedgerows and close to shrubs near the buildings. Pat Morris's studies showed that the necessary materials and places for nesting do not exist in arable fields, only around the edges, greatly restricting where hedgehogs can spend the winter.

Hedgehogs, it seems, show a preference for inhabited areas where there's more food – often supplemented by house owners putting out saucers of pet food – and more nesting places. Your garden could be very important for them. It could even save them from extinction.

MY OWN GARDEN

Hedgehogs make day roosts and they may use several of them. I always find one in the unkempt areas by the stone walls. The patch full of honeysuckle and roses, described on page 51, offers a quiet place with a ready supply of moss and beech leaves for bedding. Hedgehogs favour both materials for their day roosts. I probably have several roosts in my garden, but they are so well camouflaged that I rarely find them until everything starts to die back. However, in summer 2015 I heard a loud noise which I believed to be my neighbour erecting fence posts in the fields beyond the garden. On standing up to look and say hello, no one was about. Finally, I tracked down the heavy thump-thump to an area of the garden right against the wall a few feet from where I was sitting. It was a mossy concoction, with leaves covering a hedgehog, and I have no idea why it was making such a noise, and Pat Morris, the leading authority on hedgehogs, had no idea either. I checked it later in the dark and

I probably have several roosts in my garden, but they are so well camouflaged that I rarely find them until everything starts to die back.

found it empty, and it stayed that way for the next few days, before the hedgehog came back and occupied it again.

Day roosts are quite casual affairs, made quickly, taking roughly an hour at most. Pat Morris, in his excellent *The New Hedgehog Book*, says that in very warm weather they don't even bother to make a nest, but simply roost in 'grass tussocks or under a pile of leaves'. This makes hedgehogs very vulnerable to being strimmed, as frogs and other amphibians are. Many hedgehog rescue centres have inmates with strimming injuries to their feet or noses, so do leave those wild corners alone and learn to love them – after all, gardening is not an exercise in tidying.

> *In very warm weather they don't even bother to make a nest, but simply roost in 'grass tussocks or under a pile of leaves'.*

Winter hibernation nests, known as hibernacula, are much more elaborate. At Spring Cottage we have found several over the years. The huge stand of *Cortaderia richardii*, adjacent to the summer house, has a fountain of evergreen foliage with lots of papery debris at the base. Hedgehogs have hibernated between this and the wooden sides of the summer house. I have also found them inside a huge pile of leaves in a very sheltered position between the greenhouse and oil tank and between the cottage and the woodpile. As a result, leaves are always left to build up in these areas. Very few hedgehogs are found in treeless places, such as moorland or marsh, probably because leaves are in short supply, so do spare the leaf tidying where you can.

> *Very few hedgehogs are found in treeless places, such as moorland or marsh, probably because leaves are in short supply.*

On other occasions hedgehogs have hibernated in the autumn border on the eastern side of the summer house, in a rain shadow of the building. This border is generally cut back in late January, but if I find a winter nest it's left undisturbed until late March. Generally it's a wide mound of leafy material. Common sites are compost heaps, among brambles, under sheds, down rabbit holes, in hedge bottoms and scrubby areas. So don't 'put the garden to bed' across the board. Leave the autumn flowers intact, just removing any pernicious seed-heads from aconitums and over-enthusiastic crocosmias, for instance.

The temperature in a hibernaculum stays mainly between 1°C and 5°C, even if the temperature rises to 10°C or falls to −8°C, according to Pat Morris. His study of 180 winter nests demonstrated that hedgehogs don't return to old hibernacula. He also says that 60 per cent of hibernacula are used for two months or less, and many of us have seen or heard hedgehogs in very late autumn, suggesting that they are still feeding in the dark at this time of year.

> *You can panic if you see a hedgehog in the daytime, for these creatures are nocturnal. It could be short of food, or ill.*

They sometimes wake and move themselves during hibernation. Leave your hedgehogs to their own devices, because in theory they do not need to hibernate as long as they have plenty of food, so do not panic, and hopefully they will adapt to our warming climate.

You can panic if you see a hedgehog during the daytime in spring and summer, for these creatures are nocturnal. It could be short of food, or ill. A saucer of dog or cat food should be offered to it, along with some water. The only hedgehog discovered in my garden in daylight was making wheezy noises and the Best Beloved took it to the local refuge because it was clearly in distress. Small hedgehogs found in autumn are often taken to refuges, but Pat Morris believes that if the hedgehog weighs 450 g it can survive, so err on the side of caution before you whisk it away. It could be a female with a second litter and she could be feeding babies who will definitely perish without her.

Hedgehog droppings are abundant at Spring Cottage. They are usually found on the lawn but almost certainly present in the borders too. We hear noises during

The calling card of the hedgehog – often the only clue!

the summer months, but I will see only one or two hedgehogs a year, usually at dusk. In 2015 one was large and one was far smaller, but I can't say that they were the only hedgehogs present, or that the ones I saw more than once were actually the same ones. You can – and people do – mark hedgehogs: Pat Morris recommends quick-drying paint on the quills, either white or metallic touch-up paint used for cars. Keep it well away from the face, though.

When Pat Morris marked 'the hedgehog that visited his garden', he found that he actually had seven and that hedgehogs can visit up to 20 gardens every night. They have favoured spots and, as he says, they 'know where they are going'. I know this from my own experience, because in my old Hook Norton garden I had breeding hedgehogs. I would often see a family of hedgehogs heading towards the rather busy village street, so I kept a large cardboard box and a pair of stout gloves under my desk. I would rush out and take them to the bottom of the garden, which was a long, narrow acre. A few minutes later they would reappear, striding towards the road with real purpose, because the drive was the only way out of the garden. It was bounded by low stone walls or fenced with wire fencing. If there had been gaps through to other gardens they would not have headed for the road!

The British Hedgehog Preservation Society (www.britishhedgehogs.org.uk) recommends hedgehog gates between gardens because hedgehogs are known to set off at dusk or nightfall with a definite plan. They are able to find and re-find favoured gardens and the nests they've made. Males go further than females, striding an average of just over 1 mile a night, foraging whilst on the lookout for a mate, perhaps. Females go roughly just over ½ mile and both tend to do a circular route, often returning to their starting place. If you can prevent them crossing busy roads many more would survive because crossing roads is hazardous and, sadly, the only hedgehog many people have seen is a dead one. Their habit of rolling into a ball when stressed makes them hard to spot and they become sitting targets. May and June are the worst months. It's often males who die then, because they travel further, whereas in August it's often females having to feed families who come to grief on the roads.

Gardeners can help to keep hedgehogs safer by creating gaps in garden fences, an initiative started by Hedgehog Street, a campaign aimed at ensuring the hedgehog remains a common and familiar part of British life. You can get a special plaque that indicates why there's a gap in the bottom of the fence, so hopefully new residents won't re-block them. If you could encourage lots of neighbours to do this, it could make a huge difference. If I'd known this and opened up gaps in my Hook Norton garden, my hedgehogs could have got out of my old garden without using the drive down to the busy road. And others could have got in too.

A hedgehog gate allows access from garden to garden

The British Hedgehog Preservation Society recommends hedgehog gates between gardens because hedgehogs are known to set off at dusk or nightfall with a definite plan.

A DIET OF WORMS?

Hedgehogs are classified as insectivores, although they eat lots of other things too, and will consume up to 100 creatures per night. They are always championed as great slug eaters, but it's hard to tell this by examining their stomach contents or looking at their droppings, because slugs leave little trace behind except their radulas – the slug version of a tongue; there's no wing case, as there is with beetles.

The fullest studies on hedgehog diet were carried out by D. W. Yalden in 1976, before DNA analysis was possible. The contents of 177 hedgehog stomachs were examined under a binocular microscope, although 40 proved to be empty. Most of the hedgehogs had been trapped on an anonymous large estate in the Brecklands of Norfolk, where game birds were reared. Some insects were easy to quantify by counting wings, etc. Others, like slugs and earthworms, proved very difficult to count, although it was possible to weigh the stomach contents. On weight alone caterpillars, scarabaeid beetles (that's dung beetles and chafers) and earthworms accounted for 55 per cent of the food. Beetle remains were found in 74 per cent of the stomachs. Ground beetles (carabids) were present in 60 per cent of the stomachs. Dung beetles and chafers were present in 21 per cent and other types of beetle (mostly weevils) in 35 per cent of stomachs. Earwigs were found in 48 per cent and caterpillars in 49 per cent of stomachs. Earthworms, millipedes and slugs were also important items.

> ## GOLDEN RULE
> ------------------------------
> Give up your strimmer – they cause carnage.

The study showed that more slugs were eaten in September and October. The main prey slug was the grey field slug, a real baddie (see page 134). This small, slimy, fawn-coloured slug produces predator-deflecting slime, but hedgehogs seem immune to it. They also consumed millipedes, which birds tend to avoid owing to noxious chemicals on their skins, but chemical defence is also associated with carabids. All the hedgehogs' prey was slow-moving and easily nibbled by a small mouth. Snails, for instance, were rarely found in stomach contents, probably because they are too much of a mouthful.

Pat Morris has noticed the difference in eating noises. Hedgehogs slobber over slugs and crunch beetles, but somehow I don't fancy going out at night to listen.

A more modern look at diet, carried out by Carly Pettett in 2015, studied faecal samples from hedgehogs in north Norfolk and North Yorkshire using DNA markers. Earthworms were found in 95 per cent, 100 per cent contained beetles, 90 per cent moths and butterflies (presumably as caterpillars) and 17 per cent contained frog. Pig was also present because pet foods, often put out to supplement feeding, contain gelatine made from pigs. Rural and urban hedgehogs seemed to have very similar diets. The DNA slug marker did not work well for Carly Pettett, but it seems that slugs are consumed in numbers, especially at certain times of the year when caterpillars and beetles are not so available. In his book *Hedgehogs*, Nigel Reeve observed that mature hedgehogs have been shown to eat more earthworms because they provide more energy.

Hedgehogs must have strong stomachs, and the old wives' tale that they are immune to snake bites has been examined. It is thought that the snake's fangs are shorter than the hedgehog's spines, so the poison cannot reach the hedgehog's soft body. However, further Swedish research, quoted in Pat Morris's book, showed that hedgehog blood is less damaged by snake venom than the blood of other species. Furthermore, in hibernation hedgehogs are 'extraordinarily resistant to many poisonous substances'. Morris also adds that 'hibernation reduces metabolism, making poisons and even radiation less damaging'.

Pat Morris believes that putting out blue metaldehyde slug pellets (see pages 131–3) will kill not just slugs but also other animals, including hedgehogs. However, hedgehogs do not enjoy dry food, so probably wouldn't consume fresh pellets: they are likely to find them too hard to crunch up. Once the slug pellets become soggy they may ingest them, but by that time the active ingredient would probably have dispersed. Pat Morris's book cites a 1991 report on 74 hedgehog post-mortem examinations. Residues of the toxin were found in the liver of one, so it had been eaten and absorbed, perhaps because the hedgehog had eaten a poisoned slug.

WAYS TO HELP YOUR HEDGEHOGS

- Create some wild areas that are not disturbed.

- Leave some leaves about and don't scratch away moss. Both are good nesting materials.

- No strimming. Hedgehogs need their feet and noses!

- Don't cut down all your borders in autumn. Hedgehogs like to hibernate in these areas.

- Sign up to Hedgehog Street (www.hedgehogstreet.org) and create pathways or routes between neighbouring gardens.

- Supplement your hedgehogs' food, particularly in droughts, with pet food mixed with water. Place this under a tunnel to keep other animals away.

However, metaldehyde decomposes rapidly inside dead slugs, so poisoned dead slugs may contain little of the active ingredient. Research by Professor Schlatter on slugs and metaldehyde in Switzerland in 1976 concluded that one hedgehog would have to consume 5,000 slugs in order to be poisoned. However (as I say in my section on slugs, page 131–8), metaldehyde does pollute water courses and it is impossible to remove at the moment.

In any case, hedgehogs will clear colonies of slugs and their eggs, and most of us will feel great delight when we know we have a hedgehog, or seven, in our garden.

BEETLES

The name beetle is a corruption of the Old English *bitan* meaning little biter and they do have jaws like pliers. I can't estimate how many beetles I have in my garden, or even photograph many of them, because they scurry away far too quickly and have proved the most difficult insect of all to photograph. However, beetles are very diverse, and a famous quote by the scientist J. B. S Haldane (1892–1964) celebrates the fact: 'The Creator would appear as endowed with a passion for stars, on the one hand, and for beetles on the other, for the simple reason that there are nearly 300,000 species of beetle known, and perhaps more, as compared with somewhat less than 9,000 species of birds and a little over 10,000 species of mammals.' The number of species of beetle has risen to 350,000 since Haldane's day, but it's thought that 70–95 per cent of all beetle species still remain undescribed.

It's thought that 70–95 per cent of all beetle species still remain undescribed.

The violet ground beetle (*Carabus violaceus*) hates disturbance

Britain has 4,000 species, subdivided into 100 families, and *The State of Nature* report 2013 – a collaboration between 25 conservation and research bodies – states that many are in decline. Ground beetles (or Carabid species) were examined and almost 72 per cent showed some decrease, with 45 per cent showing a strong decrease. On farmland, 70 per cent of carabid beetles studied are declining, with few species increasing.

The State of Nature report also examined brownfield sites that were 'derelict, disused and unloved' and often ripe for redevelopment. Surprisingly, these abandoned areas often provided a much-needed refuge for important wildlife, including beetles.

Great crested newts, slow worms, common lizards and black redstarts all make their home in the mosaic of different habitats found there. Around 15 per cent of nationally rare and scarce invertebrates have been found on brownfield sites, including 50 per cent of rare solitary bees and wasps, and 35 per cent of rare carabid beetles. Brownfield sites can also support a range of important flowering plants, mosses and lichens – often including species that are declining in the wider countryside, such as the exquisite bee orchid. Studies in the Midlands suggest that the best brownfield sites even match ancient woodlands in terms of the number of species, especially rare ones, found there. The key is that they are undisturbed, and that allows nature to return.

The best brownfield sites even match ancient woodland in terms of the number of species, especially rare ones.

We are not sure how many of our 4,000 species of beetle are still to be found. Jeremy Early, in his very readable book about his own Surrey garden, *My Side of the Garden Fence*, confirms that '250 species of our almost 4000 haven't been seen since the 1970s, although they do not make their presence obvious.' Most beetles are nocturnal and at Spring Cottage I normally see them under stones or planks. This is the problem, for even those who study beetles still have much to find out owing to the difficulties of actually locating living specimens. It is trapped beetles that provide evidence of which are where, but beetles are agile little things and many probably escape from traps and pits.

However, Jennifer Owen, in *The Ecology of a Garden*, did manage to capture 14,483 beetles in her formalin traps, not including ladybirds, between 1981 and 2001. In all, 398 species of beetle in 41 different families were named.

CARABID OR GROUND BEETLES

Jennifer Owen's study reported that carabid or ground beetles formed 92.6 per cent of her total catch between 1979 and 1990. In all she found 23 species in her Leicestershire garden and it's quite likely that there could be many more in our own gardens because there are 365 carabid species in Britain. Most have long legs for extra agility and a distinct head, abdomen and thorax. Many are black.

Owen's commonest carabid beetle was *Pterostichus madidus*, which formed 68.5 per cent of her catch, because 8,644 were trapped in the 30-year period. Commonly called the black clock beetle, this shiny, black beetle measures 14–20 mm (½–¾ in) and can have all-black legs, wine-red legs or rufous-

There are 365 carabid species in Britain. Most have long legs for extra agility and a distinctive head, abdomen and thorax.

brown legs. It's known to be common in gardens, but Jennifer Owen found that numbers fluctuated from year to year, and she attributed this to lusher vegetation in damper years producing more dead and decomposing material. When I'm gardening I often lay weeds on the path or the soil before collecting them up a day or two later. The material doesn't have to be there long before some beetles have gathered under the flagging foliage.

I also see beetles under the planks that separate the vegetable beds, along with a slug or two. I suspect they make uneasy bedfellows. As winter beckons I begin to find them tucked up in grassy tussocks, although some burrow into the soil and excavate an oval chamber. In late September if I'm cutting long grass in the wild areas, using hand shears, I have to look out for them, snuggled down in the bottom of grassy tussocks.

A specialist predator of slugs, this beetle is able to prevent them from producing copious amounts of sticky mucus by paralysing them with a blow to the mantle.

Jennifer Owen also trapped 40 violet ground beetles (*Carabus violaceus*), our largest ground beetle, and these live in my garden and probably in yours too, because they're widespread in the UK, although especially associated with wooded areas. This is a relatively large beetle, around 20–30 mm (¾–1¼ in), with a bright violet sheen to its wing cases and thorax. Like most ground beetles, it's a nocturnal predator and often spends the daytime hidden under stones or logs. A specialist predator of slugs, this beetle is able to prevent them from producing copious amounts of sticky mucus by paralysing them with a bite to the mantle, the saddle-like structure on their back through which they breathe. Like all larger beetles, it needs a leafy canopy that allows its body to retain humidity, so do provide some cover.

CARABID BEETLE FACTS

- Most ground beetles are voracious predators and spend their time on the ground. Their predatory larvae are totally carnivorous, although the adults are omnivorous, sometimes eating plant material and carrion.

- Few carabids can fly, because their wing cases (elytra) are fused together to provide an armoured case.

- Many ground beetles are nocturnal, so need some form of shade during the day. Good refuges include a log pile, leaf-litter or just some large stones.

- Ground beetles can be found throughout the year, although they hibernate during the coldest winter months, sometimes in garden sheds.

A ground beetle larva dug up in the vegetable patch

Some rather ancient but pertinent laboratory research, carried out by J. W. Stephenson at Rothamsted in 1965 and cited in the excellent but out-of-print HMSO bulletin *Beneficial Insects and Mites*, looked at seven species of ground beetle and their ability to predate the grey field slug (see page 135–7). The violet ground beetle was found to be the most voracious of the seven, eating five slugs in four days, whereas *Pterostichus melanarius*, the common black ground beetle, ate five slugs in 14 days and *Abax parallelepipedus*, a beetle of moorlands and not gardens, consumed four in ten days. This may not sound like a lot of slugs, but it's quite possible that a good square metre of habitat might support many ground beetles. The figure of 60 beetles per sq. m (60 per 10½ sq. ft) has been cited.

Even older research from the then National Vegetable Research Station, where I worked as a young thing (see page 22), was carried out by R. D. Hughes and P. Salter in 1959. It demonstrated that beetles kept cabbage root fly (*Delia radicum*) at bay. Some 95 per cent of the eggs of first and second generations failed to produce adult flies during the period 1954–1958 and 90 per cent of this mortality was accounted for by beetle predation. *Bembidion lampros* was caught in pitfall traps close by and was presumably responsible.

Also at Wellesbourne, in a 1960 study D. W. Wright, R. D. Hughes and J. Worrall trapped beetles and found 60 species of rove and ground beetle on the

GENERAL BEETLE FACTS

- Beetles lay eggs in accumulations of organic matter (so please don't tidy everything away).

- Their larvae are long and soft-bodied, with three pairs of legs near the head end. The larvae generally remain in the soil, or in leaf-litter, where they feed on small invertebrates and their eggs.

- The head, thorax and usually some of the abdominal segments of larvae are often brown or black, but the underside is creamy-white.

- The adult beetles move very quickly over the soil surface.

- Most are more active at night.

Wellesbourne NVRS site. They marked their beetles and showed that little or no emigration took place, something confirmed by other studies. Once you have beetles (and a food supply of course), they should stay put. Later studies in Denmark, by Henrich Vibe Scheller in 1982–1983, looked at the guts of the ground beetles *Bembidion lampros*, *Agonum dorsale*, *Pterostichus melanarius* and *Loricera pilicornis* in spring barley fields and found aphid remains. Jennifer Owen identifies the latter two beetles in her garden.

ROVE BEETLES

A quarter of all British beetles are rove beetles, named because they are constantly on the move, and there are approximately 1,000 species belonging to the family known as the Staphylinidae. They are long and narrow with elongated bodies and short wing-cases that leave most of the abdominal segments uncovered.

The devil's coach horse (*Ocypus olens*) is the largest of our rove beetles and can reach a length of 28 mm (just over 1 in). This scorpion-like beetle is rather scary, and when I lived in rural Northamptonshire several moved indoors to an unheated outhouse once winter struck, year after year. Luckily they rarely fly, although they can, and most of the time they stayed underneath the washing machine until the spin cycle started. If threatened, the devil's coach horse raises the rear end of its body and opens its fierce jaws, looking similar to a scorpion, so it is definitely aggressive when threatened. It can also emit a foul smell from its abdominal area (*olens* means smell) via a pair of white glands, and it can squirt an unpleasant fluid from its mouth and rear.

A quarter of all British beetles are rove beetles, named because they are constantly on the move.

At night the devil's coach horse will feed on slugs, worms, spiders, woodlice, a range of other invertebrates and carrion (dead items). It turns these into balls, using its front legs, and then each ball is chewed and passes through the beetle's digestive system a number of times until it becomes liquefied and finally digested, as described on the Buglife website.

FOUR BADDIES

Not all beetles are good news and the following four are notorious pests: lily beetle, viburnum beetle, vine weevil and rosemary beetle. However, recent research shows that violet ground beetles do eat vine weevils, so they could be deployed to control these pests naturally.

Lily beetles (*Lilioceris lilii*)

This was first noticed in 1939 when a colony was recorded in a private garden at Chobham in Surrey. Since then it has spread across the country. They feed on all members of the lily family, including fritillarias, and can be spotted easily because of their red bodies. Squishing, in gloves, is the best option, but strike quickly. Once they fall they turn upside down and display a dull-brown tummy, making finding them again an impossible task. If your hearing's good, they make a noise like a boiling kettle. Their larvae are unpleasant to handle: they cover themselves in their own excrement.

Viburnum beetle (*Pyrrhalta viburni*)

The larvae of this beetle ruin the foliage of viburnums in late spring, sometimes completely defoliating whole shrubs except for the leaf veins. Female beetles chew through the bark at the tips of viburnum twigs and excavate cavities in the underlying pith. There they lay eggs in groups of about eight, covering them with frass (poo). The eggs overwinter in these cavities, protected from

The dreaded lily beetle feeding on *Fritillaria pyreniacum* in April

Vine weevil larva

An adult vine weevil. You won't know about them until your plant flags due to having no stem or roots

COMMON BEETLES IN YOUR GARDEN

Violet ground beetle (*Carabus violaceus*)
The violet ground beetle is a large inch-long (20–30 mm) beetle with violet-blue metallic sheen on the edges of the pronotum or body plate. Known to consume earthworms, slugs, snails and insects in gardens and agricultural fields.

Common black ground beetle (*Pterostichus melanarius*)
This large, black, nocturnal beetle (12–18 mm/½–¾ in) is found in all agricultural fields and gardens. Small earthworms often dominate its diet, but it also eats snails, slugs, caterpillars and aphids. Can be fond of ripe strawberries.

Black clock beetle (*Pterostichus madidus*)
This beetle is very commonly found in gardens and is known to eat caterpillars and slugs, although the adult also eats some plant material. It breeds in autumn and some adults overwinter to breed again the following summer. Another nocturnal beetle.

Hair-trap ground beetle (*Loricera pilicornis*)
A relatively small beetle (6–8 mm/just over ¼ in) that tends to inhabit wet or damp places. It's very easy to recognise by the long bristles on the first six segments of its antennae and the protruding eyes. It uses these bristles to form a sort of cage in front of its mouth to trap springtails, aphids and mites, which are its favourite prey. Very common.

Bronze carabid (*Carabus nemoralis*)
Another beetle with a metallic sheen that ranges between copper and purple, hence its common name. It consumes slugs, snails, woodlice, millipedes and centipedes.

Snail hunter beetle (*Cychrus caraboides*)
This nocturnal ground beetle feeds solely on snails when adult, and it has a narrow head and thorax to enable it to get into its prey. It is able to squirt yellow acid out of its rear end with some accuracy in order to startle any predator. It can also stridulate when picked up, using its wing cases to make a noise some describe as a squeak. The larva, which is short and fat, unlike other carabid larva, feeds mainly on slugs and snails. It is often found under rotting wood and other shaded habitats.

Nebria brevicollis
This is a large ground beetle (10–14 mm/ around ½ in) that can be black or dark brown, but with mid-brown legs and antennae. It can be confused with the very similar to *N. salina*, which prefers damper habitats. It predates small creatures. Possibly the most common British carabid, it prefers damper conditions.

The black clock beetle
(*Pterostichus madidus*)

desiccation and predators. Some Asian viburnum species, such as *V. plicatum*, are less susceptible and suffer less damage because the adults lay fewer eggs on them in the first place.

Vine weevil (*Otiorhynchus sulcatus*)

A particular pest in container-grown plants where soft, peaty compost is used. Soft, fleshy plants, such as sedums, heucheras and primroses, are most prone. Nematodes can be used in containers, and gritty compost puts them off too. They are drawn to light at night, so a wall-mounted outdoor light often lures them up a wall and makes them an easy target for the squish-squash treatment.

Rosemary beetle (*Chrysolina americana*)

An extremely pretty, small (8 mm/just over ¼ in long) metallic-green beetle with purple stripes, first found at RHS Wisley in 1994. Originally from southern Europe, this population was thought to have died away, but returned to Wisley in 2003, although it had also been seen in London and Reading in the interim. It is normally spotted feeding on rosemary or lavender, but salvia and thyme are host plants too. The larvae are grey with darker stripes and up to 8 mm (just over ¼ in) in length, hatching from sausage-shaped eggs approximately 2 mm (1/8 in) long.

FROGS, TOADS AND NEWTS

We are not overwhelmed with these at Spring Cottage because we don't have a pond. However, they do occur in the garden. The compost heap is always covered with a tarpaulin to encourage the heap to stay warm and wet for faster compost-making. Whenever it's lifted there are two toads, one darker in colour than the other and one smaller than the other. They must find plenty of food in the heap, because they seem to stay put.

There are also frogs, and the ones we have seem to divide their time between the wild area against the western wall and the strawberry bed. We also find frogs underneath the planks that divide the 2.4 × 1.2 m (8 × 4 ft) vegetable beds, so no plank is walked on without being lifted first. I'd hate to squash one! We have also found newts and once, when an old rhubarb crown was lifted, several were discovered in the hollow stems and roots.

The old garden at Hook Norton, which had two ponds, was alive with newts and once, when the pond was cleaned and dredged, we had about 100

When an old rhubarb crown was lifted, several were discovered in the hollow stems and roots.

in a single bucket. They were smooth newts. Frog, toad and newt eggs were a common sight. A garden pond is a fabulous addition to an eco-friendly garden and a great source of fascination, although the arrival of four grandchildren and lack of space has meant that we haven't made one here. This may change, as frogs and toads are declining, almost certainly due to ponds being filled in on farmland. The grandchildren are also now much larger and they can swim!

COMMON FROG (*RANA TEMPORARIA*)

Frogs and toads look rather different and, if you get close enough, you will see that frogs have a yellow iris and toads an orange one. Frogs have smooth, olive-green skin, a more aquiline shape and their stripy legs are longer. The females are larger, up to 13 cm (just over 5 in) in length. The males grow to 9 cm (just under 4 in). Both make a soft croak and are most active at night.

Frogs hibernate under rocks, in compost heaps, or under water, buried in mud and vegetation during winter. They emerge in early spring and lay globular balls of spawn, often containing up to 2,000 eggs. In this area the arrival of spawn often coincides with Valentine's Day. Small black tadpoles follow, developing light-bronze speckles as they mature. They feed on algae and water fleas to begin

Frog spawn is globular and round.
Toad spawn is long and ribbon-like

One of our resident frogs is nearly always found
under a plank close to the strawberry bed

with. After around 16 weeks the tadpoles start to grow back legs, followed by front legs. When they have fully absorbed their tails they leave the water as tiny froglets, usually in early summer but sometimes as late as September. Their diet at this stage consists of insects, slugs and worms. They reach their breeding age after two to three years and the males can be seen piggybacking their mates.

> *Frogs have good eyesight, and when they detect prey they launch themselves at it.*

Adult frogs eat snails, slugs, beetles, caterpillars, woodlice and other small animals. Frogs have good eyesight, and when they detect prey they launch themselves at it, catching it with their long, sticky tongue. They are predominantly ambush predators, waiting for moving prey to approach.

The common frog is listed as a species of least concern on the IUCN Red List of Threatened Species. However, it is declining and the use of glyphosate, a weedkiller widely used in agriculture and gardening, has been associated with the drop in numbers because they come into contact with it in their terrestrial phase. Research to assess the long-term effects is ongoing.

COMMON TOAD (*BUFO BUFO*)

Similar in size to the common frog, but the common toad has rough, 'warty' skin and tends to crawl rather than hop. They seem almost to squat on the ground, with a low profile, and, probably because they move relatively slowly, they produce a toxin from a pair of glands on their back which makes them distasteful to would-be predators. They emit a high-pitched, rough squawk that is more abrasive on the ears than a frog croak. They also prefer to breed in deeper water, including fish ponds, farm ponds, reservoirs or village ponds, and the ribbon-like spawn is arranged round plants. It's usually later than frog spawn, up to four weeks in my experience. The tadpoles stay black, with no golden speckling, unlike frog tadpoles.

Toads tend to return to ancestral breeding ponds along the same routes each year and it's quite common to see signs on the road asking drivers to slow down. The males wait near to the pond and piggyback the females as they make their way there, and I have seen rolling toad balls containing one female and a band of hopeful males.

> *Toads eat insect larvae, spiders, slugs and worms, and larger toads may even take slow worms, small grass snakes and harvest mice.*

Toads eat insect larvae, spiders, slugs and worms, and larger toads may even take slow worms, small grass snakes and harvest mice. 'The Diet of the Common

The common toad is now far from common

Toad (*Bufo bufo*) around a Pond in Mid-Wales', research carried out in 1987 by S. P. Gittins, found the diet of the toad to be very varied. The main food items were beetles, collembolans (springtails), millipedes, harvestmen and spiders. The diets of males, females and young toads were very similar, and only slight changes in diet were observed throughout the year. The size of food items ranged from 1 mm to 40 mm (up to 1½ in), with most around 7 mm (¼ in). There was no significant relationship between the size of the food item and the size of the toad for adult males and females, but there was for juveniles.

In Britain the common toad is widespread; however, populations have declined, largely due to loss of habitat. When threatened by a predator, toads will assume a defensive posture, inflating their bodies and raising themselves on their toes in an attempt to look as large as possible. Recent research has shown that in some areas crows have become adept at predating toads by pecking through the toxic skin and removing the nutritious liver. When attacked like this, the toad's diaphragm is punctured, so it has no means of controlling its inflation. This combination is fatal. Large numbers follow the same routes and are presumably easy targets, for predators and motorists, and it can often seem that numerous toads have 'exploded' in a seemingly mass mortality incident.

CREEPY CRAWLIES

SHIELD BUGS

There's something a little sci-fi about shield bugs, squat and almost rectangular, so they often make me shudder slightly when I see them on my plants. There are 1,700 species in Britain and they all have a piercing beak, rather like a syringe, that sucks out plant sap. Sounds scary, but most are fussy eaters and their common name tends to reflect their preferred food tastes. The Royal Entomological Society tells us that most shield bugs need symbiotic bacteria for the digestion of the sap. They acquire this aid to digestion at an early age, as their mother smears her eggs with the bacteria so that the young nymphs ingest them as they feed on the egg case.

They have a piercing beak, rather like a syringe, that sucks out plant sap.

Jennifer Owen, in her 30-year Leicestershire garden study, recorded 66 hawthorn shield bugs (*Acanthosoma haemorrhoidale*), 16 juniper shield bugs (*Cyphostethus tristriatus*) and 14 birch shield bugs (*Elasmostethus intersinctus*). There were also 8 parent bugs (*E. grisea*), known to feed on birch and alder. It's probable that these tree-hugging species were there in much greater numbers but were only rarely captured in her pits and traps. The charming name indicates not the shape of the insect but the parent bug's maternal habit of sitting on the eggs until they hatch; this prevents predation from parasitic wasps. The Royal Entomological Society records that shield bugs often show parental care, guarding their young from predators.

The most commonly found one at Spring Cottage is the green shield bug (*Palomena prasina*), which is a livid green in spring and summer and a dull brown in winter. Shield bugs produce one generation per year and the adults hibernate in grassy tussocks. The young wingless nymphs are born green, but then turn brown in colour, which no doubt helps them to hide in trees. They usually suck the sap of deciduous trees, typically hazel. Adults measure 10 mm (about 3/8 in) in length and they seem to bask in sunlight. Perhaps warmth is a priority, because their range is concentrated in the southern half of Britain. They are sucking sap, but in a mixed garden full of different species and types of plant

Shield bugs mating on achillea

Earwigs do eat your aphids

any damage is minimal and should be tolerated. Their tasty little nymphs must
be feeding lots of predators, from birds downwards.

EARWIGS

The earwig is not a popular garden insect – perhaps its scorpion-like shape and
fast-moving gait inspire panic rather than affection. I know I have plenty. A
handful of spinach, a few ears of sweetcorn or a
bunch of dahlias inevitably contains some earwigs.
And dahlia enthusiasts go to great lengths to stop
them 'chobbling' the petals and leaves. Most serious
growers use inverted pots, filled loosely with dried
grass or straw. It's dry and warm, and your earwigs

*On the plus side, earwigs do play
a beneficial role in the garden by
attacking pests such as aphids.*

see it as The Ritz, making them easy to collect and destroy should you wish to.
Earwigs can damage fruit too, allowing the entry of fungal diseases.

However, on the plus side, earwigs do play a beneficial role in the garden by
attacking pests such as aphids, so I allow these omnivores to get on with it.

Their Latin family name, *Dermaptera*, refers to their skin-like wings, although
they rarely fly. There are four species in Britain, the commonest being *Forficula
auricularia*. They are nocturnal and seek out dark crevices, easing their way into

GOLDEN RULE

If you find clusters of eggs during winter, leave them alone. They are more likely to be helpful predators than pests. I've never killed a spider, even the one that bit me when I was picking runner beans in the so-called summer of 2015. Quite a nip.

the husks of sweetcorn, for instance. Female earwigs are good mothers. They lay 20–30 eggs and protect them through the winter. When they hatch, they feed and tend the nymphs until they are able to fend for themselves. Again, it's just one generation per year, so show them some humanity.

SPIDERS
I have a soft spot for spiders that began in the early 1970s when I rented a flat in Leamington Spa. It just happened to be next to a huge fruit warehouse owned by Griffin and Steele, so I found that my flat had more than its fair share of spiders – big and hairy ones, and possibly not British either. Luckily I was able to arm myself with lots of jam jars and postcards, which I arranged on my mantelpiece as tastefully as any ornaments. I became adept at trapping them and walking them further up the street. The old Victorian building of the long-gone fruit firm is now retirement apartments, hopefully spider-free.

Jeremy Early, writing in *My Side of the Fence*, tells us that there are 600 species of spider in Britain and probably 100 of these could be found in gardens. Jennifer Owen found 80 different species in her garden, but she needed a great deal of help to identify them. Jeremy writes that 'most catch invertebrates that are viewed as pests, and provide food for birds along with nest building substances via their webs'. So when I visit any garden I actively look for spiders, as these predators indicate a healthy ecosystem and a chemical-free regime. They're a little like a natural garden barometer, because these sensitive, soft-bodied creatures are soon knocked out by pesticides.

The most obvious and commonly found spider in the garden is the garden cross spider (*Araneus diadematus*). Its presence is most noticeable in autumn when the huge dew-lined orb webs festoon strong-stemmed plants and hedges. I can remember walking through suburban London in the 1950s counting web after web on my way to school in misty, moist autumn weather.

My flat had more than its fair share of spiders – big and hairy ones, and possibly not British either.

I occasionally pushed a finger through one span of the sticky web so that the spider shot forwards and trembled and sometimes began an immediate repair. Most spinning takes place during the night so that the web is fully primed for

An unknown spider on a hemerocallis, with prey

the following day to catch flying insects such as butterflies, wasps, bees and flies – although I've seen all manner of things in webs, including ladybirds.

The garden spider has a distinctive white cross on its back, although the overall body colour can vary from light brown, to reddish-brown to black. An adult female will grow to 15 mm (about ½ in), with males reaching only 9 mm (about 1/3 in). Both sexes are mature in late summer and autumn, with the females surviving through to late autumn, when the frost kills them. The eggs will already have been laid in a silk egg sac, which the female protects until she dies. Her 'spiderlings' hatch in the following May, and you often see bundles of tiny, gold-tinted spiders clinging together in this month, each the size of a pinhead. It takes two years for the young spiderlings to reach maturity in Britain, and immatures may be found throughout the year.

At Spring Cottage we find more spiders in the long grass than anywhere else. These areas are cut only once, by hand in late August or September, and this must save the life of many a spider. It's quite understandable, because a single acre of hay meadow is estimated to contain 2.25 million spiders. Each of these will eat two insects a week for six months, which works out at about 108 million insects! Log piles and compost heaps also attract plenty of spiders.

MICE, VOLES AND SHREWS

We seem to have lots of small rodents here, probably owing to our wild areas and all the cracks and crevices in the drystone walls. I know where my rodent-rich areas are because Poppy Cat stalks them ruthlessly and often strikes lucky. Too well fed to eat them, she abandons their bodies once her playful side has been satisfied, patting them about like Andy Murray in a long rally. She catches small rodents rather than rats, which we also have at times. Any garden that has a chicken coop will attract rats. On the plus side, rats do eat slugs and snails.

YELLOW-NECKED MICE

Mice can be a nuisance in the garden, as anyone who has watched a row of peas disappear can vouch. I don't trap my garden mice, as I am never sure which mouse has sinned. However, I have to use mouse traps in two places in the house – the pantry and the airing cupboard. One's full of food and one's exceptionally warm. The pantry traps led to the killing of several yellow-necked mice (*Apodemus flavicollis*) one year. These lovely, doe-eyed creatures, with Mickey Mouse ears and charm, have golden-brown fur with a yellow band on their throats. They are not common everywhere, being concentrated into areas around the Welsh borders, the western Cotswolds and the south-eastern counties. It's estimated that there's a breeding population of 750,000, so they are not endangered – except in my pantry. They have a life span of 12–24 months, so very few survive two winters running.

They have a life span of 12–24 months, so very few survive two winters running.

Our yellow-necked mice probably live in an undisturbed area to the north of our cottage which we don't own. They nest below ground, under the stumps or roots of trees, and their nests consist of a ball of dry grass, moss and leaves. Their diet is varied and includes seedlings, buds, fruit, nuts, insects, larvae and spiders.

Wood mouse

They store food underground in burrows, or occasionally in disused bird nests which they scramble up to. They are excellent climbers and collect seeds from trees, and we are surrounded by beech trees that seem to produce beech masts nine years out of ten. Sometimes I find a cache under the bonnet of my car.

WOOD MICE

I know we have wood mice (*Apodemus sylvaticus*), also known as the long-tailed field mouse. This is smaller in size, roughly 8–10 cm (up to 4 in), with darker, duller fur and smaller eyes and ears. The varied omnivorous diet includes nuts, berries, seeds, acorns, haws, fungi, spiders and rose hips, as well as small insects and larvae. They will also eat invertebrates, worms, carrion (dead animal carcasses) and other similar things. Food is stored in underground burrows or occasionally in disused bird nests. They are a vital source of food for other larger nocturnal hunters, particularly owls, and we have barn and tawny owls close to the garden. Some bumblebees nest in old mouse nests.

Food is stored in underground burrows or occasionally in disused bird nests.

VOLES

Field voles (*Microtus agrestis*) inhabit my airing cupboard, and I also have traps there, out of necessity. I had a whole family one year, chewing my towels and devouring my Imperial Leather soap, whilst ignoring the lavender and blocks of Pears soap. They are grey to yellow-brown and have straighter bodies than mice, almost mole-like in shape to my thinking, and blunter noses. Their tails make up a third of their body length, so they are known as short-tailed voles. In all, they measure 9–13 cm (3½–5 in) long and weigh 18–60 g (roughly ½–2 oz). Their eyes are set in either side of their head, giving them a wide field of vision.

Field voles prefer mainly open, grassy habitats with dense ground cover and Poppy Cat often catches them in the wild areas where there's plenty of tussocky grass. They enjoy eating grass stems and green leaves, but in winter they will devour roots, bulbs and bark. They often dig up crocus bulbs here, but again they're discerning: they selected a lovely purple-and-grey crocus named 'Yalta', ignoring the others.

They enjoy eating grass stems and green leaves, but in winter they will devour roots, bulbs and bark.

Voles are active by day and night, and Poppy Cat frequently catches one in the afternoon. We have vole years, when many corpses appear, and years where we have far fewer. These spikes in populations usually occur every three to five years. A recent population estimate put the number of field voles in Britain at 75 million, but they are important food for owls and other proper predators

Bank vole

who depend on them for sustenance, rather than as playful distraction. Kestrels and weasels are their other main predators. They are also aggressively territorial, and a resident vole will attack and even kill another vole trespassing on its patch.

They are also aggressively territorial, and a resident vole will attack and even kill another vole trespassing on its patch.

Bank voles (*Clethrionomys glareolus*) are smaller and redder in colour, with ears that are so small you can hardly see them. Their tails are longer than those of the field vole, making up 50 per cent of their body length. In all they measure 8–12 cm (3–4¾ in) in length and weigh 15–40 g (½–1½ oz). Their diet consists mostly of plant material, including green leaves, seeds, fruits and small amounts of fungi, roots, flowers and moss. They are very

A shrew is small, with a pointed nose that's perfect for foraging for insects

keen on hazelnuts and blackberries, which we have here. Although the squirrels generally get the hazel nuts first.

Voles make tracks through long grass to avoid predators such as owls and kestrels. When I'm cutting my mini-meadow in late August or September, there are always vole runs in the grass. They are most active after dark, but they usually have several short periods of activity throughout the day too. Bank voles are also gregarious and large populations can occur in small areas where the environment is suitable.

Bank voles are also gregarious and large populations can occur in small areas where the environment is suitable.

SHREWS

In our garden we also find the bodies of shrews, tiny little mammals with long pointed noses, tiny eyes, small ears and red teeth. Although I must say I have not examined their teeth. Their small bodies have whitish fur on the underside, dark fur on the back and paler-brown on the sides, and it has a velvety texture. They measure 48–80 mm (1¾–3 in), and weigh 5–14 g (1/5–½ oz).

I am always very sad when I find a shrew, because they are insectivores and consume insects, earthworms, small slugs and snails, especially in damp areas. I find collections of undamaged snail shells on the damp side of our boundary walls and believe they have been devoured by shrews.

Shrews do not hibernate, but they do become less active in the winter months. Remarkably, their size shrinks in winter, so they require less effort to move and so need less food. Not only does the liver shrink, but also the brain and the skull. They are most commonly killed by tawny owls and barn owls, although weasels, foxes, stoats and kestrels have all been observed as predators. They are often found abandoned by the predator, particularly cats, since a liquid produced from glands on the skin is foul-tasting. Shrews are noted for providing a home for a large number of parasites, normally transmitted to the shrew from its prey.

Their size shrinks in winter, so they require less effort to move and so need less food.

Shrews are highly territorial and socialise with one another only in the mating season. Females have three or four litters of from five to seven young between May and September. Females are promiscuous, so a litter may have two or three different fathers. Young shrews are occasionally observed following their mother in a 'caravan', each grasping the base of the tail of the shrew in front, so that the mother runs along with a line of young trailing behind. This behaviour is often associated with disturbance of the nest, but may also be used to encourage the young to explore their environment.

Females are promiscuous, so a litter may have two or three different fathers.

Unfortunately, I've never been privy to this sight, and the presence of a cat is not to be encouraged when it comes to rodents. On the upside, Poppy Cat rarely catches a bird.

Geum 'Totally Tangerine' in May

CHAPTER 12

TOP 100 PLANTS FOR AN ECO-FRIENDLY GARDEN

10 WOODY PLANTS FOR PERMANENT STRUCTURE

These will give the garden scale, offer overhead shelter and drain the ground.

Hawthorn (*Crataegus mongyna*)
Hedges are much better than fences and this native will provide fruit and nesting sites for birds, plus flowers for pollinators. In theory, it could also attract 149 species of insect in Britain – it's fourth behind oak (284), willow (266) and birch (229).

Daphne laureola
A British native 'winter-warmer' evergreen with high-gloss green foliage and limy-green flowers in spring. These are fly- and moth-pollinated. It's compact, fairly small, but will provide shelter for small birds and mammals in winter. Berries follow. Its great advantage – an ability to thrive in shade.

Hazel (*Corylus avellana*)
Hazel can either be grown as a specimen shrub in woodland, or added to a hedge. Catkins appear in spring and nuts follow. It could attract 79 species of insect in Britain and sticks can be cut in winter for staking.

Apple (*Malus domestica*)
Incorporating an apple tree or two into your garden works on many levels. The blossom is highly attractive to bees and the good apples feed you. The windfalls sustain birds and you could attract 93 species of insects too.

Lonicera × purpusii 'Winter Beauty' AGM
Its sweetly scented flowers can appear as early as January and any early-flying bees are very grateful. A little scruffy in summer, though.

Prunus 'Kursar'
A reliable, easy-flowering ornamental cherry that's perfect for the smaller garden. The graceful branches are clothed with early-March, almond-pink flowers that are adored by bees. Good autumn colour and shape.

Viburnum × bodnantense 'Dawn' AGM
A large shrub with an upright habit, so relegate it to a boundary or edge. Hyacinth-scented flowers appear between late-autumn and spring, whenever the weather is clement.

Buxus sempervirens 'Suffruticosa'
Box, a British native, is mostly trimmed and topiarised for its winter presence. Ladybirds and other insects shelter in the foliage in spring, a halfway house that seems also to shelter early aphids or possibly whitefly.

Ilex aquifolium 'Handsworth New Silver' AGM
English hollies are mostly dioecious, with male and female flowers on separate bushes. Red berries are abundant on the female 'Handsworth New Silver' until the birds strip them in December. The neat silvery variegation and pyramidal shape are pleasing.

Pyracantha 'Orange Glow' AGM
These autumn berries will be the first to disappear, devoured by thrushes, blackbirds and flocks of finches that may include blackcaps and siskins. Less invasive than cotoneaster and superb trained on to a wall.

Apple blossom is a great bee pleaser in spring

Daphne bholua 'Jacqueline Postill'

10 EARLY BEE PLANTS

Essentials for the first bees, who need emergency supplies of nectar and pollen.

- -

Clematis cirrhosa **var.** *purpurascens* 'Freckles' AGM
Needs a south-facing wall, like all forms of *C. cirrhosa*. 'Freckles' is the earliest to flower, often in November, with white bells heavily spotted in red. Do not prune.

Helleborus × hybridus **(hybrid hellebores)**
Appearing from February, with rounded flowers formed by weather-resistant tepals rather than petals. Full of nectar and pollen for the first few weeks and then the tepals remain for two months or so – still looking like flowers.

Narcissus **'W. P. Milner'**
Simply bred daffodils, close to wild type, are far more attractive to bees than elaborately bred doubles. The best native is *N. pseudonarcissus* subsp. *pseudonarcissus*. 'W. P. Milner', a swept-back daffodil in buttermilk and lemon, is an old Backhouse variety from 1884 that has a wild look.

Crocus sieberi **subsp.** *sublimis* 'Tricolor' AGM
An enduring small crocus – and so many aren't – with the ability to flower early. Small, goblet-shaped purple, white and egg-yolk-yellow flowers trap warm air, making nectar flow – even when there's snow on the ground. Any crocus will do, though!

Rosmarinus **'Miss Jessop's Upright'** AGM
A very upright, aromatic rosemary with lavender-blue flowers. Give it a warm site, or place it close to a sunny wall, and this will flower with the first crocus. Adored by bees.

Daphne bholua **'Jacqueline Postill'** AGM
This Himalayan species needs a warm, sheltered site or hard winters will cut it back. A columnar evergreen with waxy, highly fragrant blue-pink flowers held in tight clusters.

Primula **'Barbara Midwinter'**
A yellow-eyed, bright-pink primrose supported by green, crinkle-edged foliage that shows its affiliation to *Primula juliae*, a primrose from the eastern Caucasus. Tuck it close to a box ball and it will flower from November until March. All primulas and primroses are good news.

Scilla siberica **AGM**
Cobalt-blue flowers, usually in March, attract many bees, who pack the steely-blue pollen into their sacs. Seeds follow and in time *S. siberica* forms useful carpets in shady places.

Galanthus elwesii **AGM**
This substantial snowdrop with wide, grey-green leaves produces single white flowers that are boldly marked in dark green. It prefers a more open site, tends to flower early and will attract bees and may set seeds.

Eranthis hyemalis **(winter aconite)** AGM
A herald of spring that needs a well-drained and warm site. If you can establish some of these globe-shaped flowers, which only open at 10°C, they will be a magnet for early pollinators. Seed follows.

10 PLANTS FOR BORDERS AND EDGES

The outer edges of the garden are perfect for these because they can survive in areas that don't get disturbed.

Lonicera periclymenum

This is our wild woodbine, a plant with long-trumpeted flowers designed for the long proboscises of butterflies and moths. It is highly fragrant in the evenings and, once pollinated, produces luscious berries which are normally eaten by blackbirds in autumn. It's a good scrambler with roses, but takes time to establish.

Rosa glauca AGM

A wild-looking shrub rose, suitable for poorer soils, with smoky, grey-green foliage. The insignificant pink-and-white flowers are followed by small hips that seem to hover between cocoa and plum as they develop. These are adored by birds, including tits and finches. Produces seedlings.

Vinca difformis 'Jenny Pym'

A tall vinca, or periwinkle, with full pink flowers edged and centred in white between autumn and winter with good green foliage. All periwinkles will do well against walls, but *V. minor* can be invasive and produce a network of runners. 'Jenny Pym' is easier to control.

Dipsacus fullonum (wild teasel)

This statuesque, spiny plant is only for the tolerant, because it will self-seed and place its strong, bright-green rosettes where not wanted. However, if you can tolerate its habits, it's great for bees in June and is a goldfinch lure in autumn and winter. The leaves cup water, too, where they join the stem, and many birds drink from these 'birdbaths'.

Symphytum × uplandicum 'Bocking 14'

This non-seeding, sterile comfrey raised by Henry Doubleday at Bocking in Essex still has the same nectar-rich flowers as other comfreys, but you won't get seedlings, just happy bees. As with many of the borage family, the nectar is continually replenished. Long-tongued bees feed properly, but those with shorter tongues bite into the back. A good accelerator for the compost heap – just add a layer of chopped-up leaves – and this one makes the best comfrey tea.

Pulmonaria 'Diana Clare' AGM

I tend to restrict all pulmonarias to edges because they self-seed too enthusiastically, however hard I try to dead-head them after flowering. This one is my desert island pulmonaria, with violet flowers above apple-green leaves. Don't shear this one back – it resents it. Other good pulmonarias include the narrow-leaved blue 'Ankum', with heavily spotted foliage, and the brick-red 'Leopard', which looks as though someone has rolled a silver die (or dice) over the foliage.

Valeriana officinalis

This highly scented plant has umbel-like domes of flowers in pink and white, held on strong, upright stems above divided foliage. Flowering in June, it's very popular with flies and hoverflies, and the lily-like scent is extraordinary.

Geranium 'Patricia' AGM

This large, magenta-pink hardy geranium needs space, but the sterile flowers go on for months and still attract the bees, although it can't set seeds.

Pulmonaria 'Diana Clare'

Digitalis lutea

This slender foxglove is a true perennial, living for many years in shady corners close to the walls here. The small, yellow flowers, held on tapering heads, appear in summer, pleasing the bees, and seeds follow.

Euphorbia palustris AGM

Easy to establish in wilder areas, especially if they are slightly damp, this summer-flowering euphorbia dies down in winter before producing plentiful rosettes of foliage topped with acid-yellow flowers and bracts.

10 ANNUALS AND BIENNIALS

Annuals and biennials have to set seed to survive and as a result they are very rich in nectar. Collect your own seeds and sow them in the following spring, or allow them to self-seed from autumn onwards.

Centaurea cyanus
Taller blue forms of this British cornfield annual are the best plant I know for red-tailed bumblebees. Dead-headed, it will stay in flower for months. Sow early in trays, prick out and pot on for the best results.

Scabiosa atropurpurea
The annual scabious, which peaks in midsummer, attracts bees for many months if dead-headed. Colours vary from almost black through to pink and white. There are annual blue forms too and perennial ones, such as *S. columbaria*. Any form of scabious is welcome. Collect seeds, sow in March, prick out and pot on.

Calendula officinalis
This annual pot marigold will self-seed happily. Go for single forms, such as 'Indian Prince', and these will attract hoverflies and bees of every type. Will flower late into the year.

Cosmos bipinnatus
This Mexican annual is easily grown and performs better once the days begin to shorten. It's superb between August and October, producing flowers late into the year. Look for single forms rather than head-heavy doubles and semi-doubles. Collect seeds, sow in March, prick out and pot on.

Eryngium giganteum AGM
This silvery architectural biennial sea holly is best left to self-seed. If you wish to restrict it, cut off most of the thimbles as they fade to pale brown – but not all. It is beloved of bumblebees, particularly buff-tailed bumblebees.

Tropaeolum majus (nasturtium)
The huge, caper-like seeds of this frost-tender annual should be sown direct in early May for summer flowers in sunshine shades of yellow, red and orange. The spurred varieties are more nectar-rich and the trailing varieties probably better than the compact form when it comes to attracting bees. The flowers are edible, once the pollen beetles decamp.

Borago officinalis
This somewhat scruffy annual has starry blue flowers that draw in the bees, because this plant can replenish its nectar within minutes. Mingle it among orange calendulas and nigella. The leaves and flowers of the borage are edible. Self-seeds.

Tagetes erecta
The foot-high African marigold varieties 'Mr Majestic' and 'Tall Scotch Prize' mingle well with other annuals and, being orange and single, these pull in loads of insects including hoverflies. When young, the plants attract every slug in the area – so you can use them as slug magnets for a nighttime – well dusk actually – massacre.

Salvia viridis (clary)
This easy annual has a long presence in the garden because the 'flowers' consist of bracts rather than petals. Sets seeds and comes in blue, white and pink with sage-like foliage.

Phacelia tanacetifolia
Often sold as a green manure, this easy, grey-blue hardy annual seems to come into its own in the summer evenings, when honeybees feast on the nectar.

Annuals and biennials are the most bee-friendly plants of all. *Eryngium giganteum* has a statuesque presence

10 GAP PLANTS FOR MAY

Plugging the nectar gap between spring and summer perennials.

Verbascum phoeniceum '**Violetta**'

This slender, April-flowering verbascum comes in three colours. 'Violetta' is a vivid purple, 'Rosetta' a carmine pink and 'Flush of White' a blush white. 'Violetta' seems the strongest, returning year after and producing a small rosette of crinkled green leaves. Like all rosettes, this can shelter insects. The long wand of flowers keeps going over many months and it self-seeds, if left, without being threatening. Rosettes and spires are generally excellent providers of nectar and pollen-flowers. Flowers on a stick.

Lamprocapnos spectabilis (**formerly** *Dicentra spectabilis*) **AGM**

This is the pink-and-white bleeding heart, with tall, arching stems and pink hearts. Although said to be pollinated by bugs and beetles, I've watched bumblebees force open the pink outer petals to reach the pollen-rich stamens. It flowers in April and can be flattened by frost, so place it somewhere clement in good soil. Good with late tulips.

Hesperis matronalis

Sweet rocket or dame's violet are two of the names for this tall, self-seeding, short-lived perennial that hovers between silver and mauve. Named hesperis, after the evening star, for its ability to glow in evening light, the fragrance deepens in the evening in order to attract moths – although bees visit too. A brassica with four-petalled flowers, it forms long, slender seed pods and will self-seed. Cut the stems off after flowering if you find self-seeders threatening.

Geranium phaeum

This early-flowering hardy geranium will grow in shade and still attract the bees. Seeds follow and in summer finches will arrive and gobble them up. 'Samobar' has dark flowers and darkly zoned foliage, and 'Rose Madder' has brown-pink flowers and plain-green foliage. Other early-flowering hardy geraniums include forms of *G. macrorrhizum* 'White-Ness', the bright-pink 'Czakor' and the pale-pink 'Ingwersen's Variety'. These sprawl and bear aromatic foliage that's questionably pleasant.

Polemonium '**Northern Lights**'

This is a sterile, very sweetly scented and nectar-rich form of Jacob's ladder which flowers over many weeks, pleasing the bees. 'Lambrook Mauve' is a pale-mauve form, sterile, with a distinct orange eye. Non-sterile forms that set seed include 'Purple Rain', *P. pulcherrimum* and *P. caeruleum*. The ferny foliage and the upright stem of flowers are attractive – although seedlings pop up regularly.

Lunaria rediviva **AGM**

The perennial honesty begins to flower in May and then the phlox-like heads develop into a mound of lilac and silver flowers set off by bright-green serrated foliage. It's long-flowering and probably more attractive to moths, and seed pods can follow. They are slender ovals, rather than the round pennies found on *Lunaria annua*, and rarely produce seedlings.

Viola cornuta **AGM**

The winged violet is perennial, with wispy flowers that appear in flushes between early May and September. Plants need to be sheared back in September to nothing, so that they form a tight mat of foliage able to withstand winter. 'Alba' is a pure white, good in shade, and 'Belmont Blue' is the most perennial of all.

Perennial honesty makes May very special

Lamium orvala

The square stems of this plant indicate that it's a labiate and this is a bee-pleasing family. *L. orvala* is plum-pink deadnettle with attitude and presence, and the huge flowers with heavily spotted lips are equalled by handsome, nettle-like foliage – but without a sting.

Allium hollandicum 'Purple Sensation' AGM

This tall, purple allium, which is easy and cheap, is the perfect follow-up act for later tulips. Flowering from May, it's a real bee-pleaser, but does set seed, so cut away the stems just before the black seeds escape. This will allow the bulb to flower well for five years or so – although flowers size shrinks.

Aquilegia vulgaris

Aquilegia flowers come in singles and doubles and both are insect friendly. Seeds do not generally come true, but there a few stable forms which do come true from seed (or virtually true). They include the green-tipped white single 'Munstead White', the quilled green-and-pink 'Nora Barlow', the pied black-and-white 'William Guinness' and the double 'Ruby Port'. Seedlings can be a problem, and a haircut before winter is advisable to encourage new foliage in very early spring.

Bupleurum fruticosum is one of the few shrubby umbellifers

10 UMBELS

Tiny, dainty flowers, usually in pallid colours, that particularly suit hoverflies with small mouths.

- -

Astrantia 'Roma' AGM

A strong-pink sterile astrantia with a ring of neat bracts surrounding a nosegay of individual flowers. Begins in May and goes on late, and there are no unwanted seedlings.

Orlaya grandiflora

Perhaps the most decorative annual umbellifer of all, this Mediterranean species has a lace-cape arrangement of tiny flowers surrounded by large white florets. The foliage is grey and finely divided – but it's usually found in some shade in the wild, often close to olive groves. Allow most of the oval barbed seeds to fall, then sow the remaining few as soon as they are ripe.

Eryngium × zabelii

So hard to choose one sea holly, but this old hybrid comes in some lovely forms. 'Big Blue', for instance, has dark-blue stems topped with electric-blue flowers consisting of an oval thimble surrounded by a ragged star of bracts. The bees and hoverflies adore it.

Cenolophium denudatum

Known as the Chelsea cow parsley for its ability to flower during Chelsea week, this billowing Russian and north Asian umbellifer bears white, domed heads set above deep-green divided foliage. Likes a cool spot and is just as lovely in fresh green bud as in flower.

Chaerophyllum hirsutum 'Roseum'

A chervil with lilac-pink flowers that appear in May, looking like a wilding but so suitable for early spring. Needs good soil.

Selinum wallichianum AGM

Named the Queen of the Umbellifers by E. A. Bowles, because it's tall and statuesque, with the best foliage of all, like green lace. The bloomed-purple sheathing to the stems and the large heads of white flowers, almost eupatorium-like, appear here in August.

Ammi visnaga

An annual that bears a lot of resemblance to our wild carrot because it gathers up its seed head into a witch's besom in autumn. Ferny, carrot-like foliage and a compact habit make it a good border plant. I find *A. majus*, another tap-rooted annual, a little floppy. Sow in autumn or early spring and prick out early or sow direct. Allow both to shed their seeds.

Anthriscus sylvestris 'Raven's Wing'

A dark form of our native cow parsley that produces 50 per cent dark seedlings and 50 per cent green-leaved ones. These helpfully show their colour immediately. Good in wilder places in the garden.

Bupleurum fruticosum

August can be such a drab, dry month, so any plant that looks as fresh as home-made lemonade is welcome. This shrubby umbellifer, one of a very few woody ones, produces a large roundel of grey-green foliage topped by lime-green heads of flower. Irresistible to flies – who are excellent pollinators.

Bupleurum rotundifolium 'Griffithii'

A 30 cm (1 ft) high annual with grey-green foliage and heads that have jagged grey bracts surrounding lime-yellow flowers. A wonderful foil for orange annuals, a great cut flower and an insect magnet.

10 NECTAR PLANTS FOR BUTTERFLIES AND MOTHS

These need to be planted in warm, sheltered locations so that the nectar flows.
If they attract butterflies they will also attract bees.

Matthiola incana **f.** *alba*

The grey-leaved sea stock needs a warm, dry site and it needs to be dead-headed because if left to seed it will die. Cut off the spent flowers as they fade. Its scented white flowers attract moths, bees and early butterflies and it blooms from late spring onwards. Because it's a member of the Brassica family, it can be attacked by cabbage white caterpillars.

Lathyrus latifolius **AGM**

A perennial sweet pea with non-fragrant flowers. This flowers in summer and can scramble through a buddleia or other shrub. Do not allow the pods to ripen because the seedlings could overrun you. The bright-pink form is adored by brimstone butterflies. It's a very good cut flower too.

Origanum laevigatum '**Herrenhausen**' **AGM**

Origanums and many aromatic herbs have sugar-packed nectar, and this August-flowering plant bears two-tone pink-and-purple sprays that are hardly ever without a small tortoiseshell or small copper butterfly.

Centranthus ruber

Valerian, which comes in pink, red and white, is one of the best plants for butterflies and moths, because it will flower in April when brimstones and orange-tips abound, and then carry on throughout summer. Cut back in July, to the ground, it will then go on to produce late-autumn flowers too. Beloved of the humming-bird hawk-moth, it can be kept in flower for months when dead-headed. The Moroccan valerian, *C. lecoqii*, hovers between pink and blue and has proved hardy. All self-seed.

Hummingbird hawk-moth on valerian

Not all sedums are insect-friendly, but 'Purple Emperor' is a high-summer favourite

Verbena bonariensis AGM

This willowy verbena, originally from Buenos Aires, is a butterfly lure in late summer. Easy to grow and capable of self-seeding, its upright slender presence and flat-topped flowers, which provide landing platforms, is always welcome in a border, providing weeks of nectar.

Phlox paniculata

The summer-flowering border phlox smells of sweet cake and meadows, and this makes it attractive to butterflies. Good forms include these two pinks, 'Eva Cullum' AGM and 'Monica Lynden-Bell' AGM, and the lilac 'Franz Schubert' AGM. Dead-head to get more flower and cut back early in autumn to discourage stem eelworm.

Symphyotrichum novae-angliae (New England asters)

These stiff-stemmed, September-flowering asters peak in butterfly season. They are easy to grow, mildew-resistant and, unlike many, do not need very regular division. Good forms include the purple 'Helen Picton', 'Harrington's Pink' AGM, 'Barr's Pink', and 'Rosa Sieger' AGM.

Buddleja 'Lochinch' AGM

The buddleia is the best plant for sustaining British butterflies, despite hailing from China. In theory it can attract 22 species and at Spring Cottage 9 species have been recorded. All forms of *B. davidii* are excellent, regardless of colour, I've found. However, 'Lochinch', a hybrid between *B. davidii* and *B. fallowiana*, has refined silvery foliage and lavender flowers with large, orange eyes. This graceful shrub retains leaf in winter and is less ungainly.

Erysimum 'Bowles' Mauve' AGM

A sterile perennial wallflower with grey foliage and mauve flowers that appear for many months of the year, beginning early. Sustains early-flowering butterflies. Trim back in midsummer to keep it compact.

Thyme (*Thymus*)

This low-growing herb comes in many forms, usually producing pink flowers in summer. It's very useful at the front of a sunny border, or grown in paving cracks. Small coppers, blues and small tortoiseshells adore thymes as do bees.

10 HIGH-SUMMER NECTAR PLANTS

Nectar isn't standard issue. It varies in sugar content and plants often regulate their supply by switching off the nectar in different ways. The following plants have plenty.

Malva moschata **(musk mallow)**
The white-and-pink saucers of this plant boost the nectar at midday to attract bumblebees and butterflies. Honeybees find the pollen of malvas unacceptable. This does self-seed and the seedlings take some weeding out!

Geranium × riversleaianum **'Mavis Simpson'**
A low, prostrate, pale-pink hardy geranium that is never without a bee. It will flower from May onwards and, if given a sunny well-drained position, it should come through the winter year after year.

Sedum telephium **(Atropurpureum group) 'Purple Emperor' AGM**
The best-behaved sedum because it doesn't set seeds or need constant division. The foliage is satin-sheened and dusky from the word go and the ruby-red second-half-of-summer flowers attract bees in large numbers.

Verbascum chaixii **'Album'**
Thin tapers of small white flowers with orange anthers, blotched in berry shades in the middle, on a truly perennial plant. Good grey-green foliage and the perfect partner for roses in shades of pink and purple-pink. All verbascums are good nectar plants, but few are long-lived. This one is!

Agastache **'Blackadder'**
More persistent for me than 'Blue Fortune', and I prefer its more slender blue tapers with black overtones rather than thicker, pale-blue bottlebrushes. Very nectar-rich, as many aromatic plants are.

Lavandula angustifolia **'Melissa Lilac'**
Any form of English lavender will do for the bees, but this one is a lilac-blue with flowers that bear a ring of petals.

Nepeta grandiflora **'Bramdean'**
The catmints are all attractive to pollinators, but this one is more upright, with deeper-blue flowers held in bluer calices (bud cases). In dry weather the stems and foliage darken to thunderclouds – and it doesn't flop all over everything else.

Scabiosa columbaria
A small scabious, a British native, which has a pincushion of flowers in the middle topped by stamens. Irresistible to all pollinators and much more garden-friendly than the field scabious (*Knautia arvensis*).

Centaurea dealbata **'Steenbergii'**
Cornflowers are wonderful bee plants. This rose-pink one, known as the Persian cornflower, flowers from June until September and possibly later – in flushes. The foliage is grey-green and deeply divided.

Digitalis purpurea
Our native biennial foxglove produces a spike of cowl-shaped flowers in midsummer and these come in shades of pink, white and apricot, some with heavy spotting. Bees begin at the bottom and work their way up to the nectar source, pollinating as they go. Lots of seeds and they germinate in light positions – never quite where you want them. Useful wintergreen rosettes.

Verbascum chaixii 'Album' – a reliably perennial
verbascum with slender tapers

The herbaceous clematis 'Cassandra' is an autumn magnet for pollinators

10 LATE PERFORMERS

Keeping the show going through the crystal-clear light of autumn will provide
late sustenance for your bees and other pollinators.

Rudbeckia triloba AGM
A branching, short-lived perennial with small yellow
flowers button-eyed in rich brown. Often still going
in November. Self-seeds in warm gardens.

Kniphofia rooperi AGM
Normally the latest poker, with conical orange
flowers that appear any time between September
and late October, depending where you live. Good
with golden grasses and late blue aconitums.

Aconitum carmichaelii 'Arendsii' AGM
Self-supporting, downy-stemmed, rich-blue
aconitum that performs in September. The good
foliage, almost always missing with this genus, is a
bonus. Dead-head to prevent seedlings and do be
aware that all aconitums are toxic.

Verbena macdougalii
Seek out this tall verbena for its strong, ribbed
stems cloaked in small lavender flowers. Taller than
V. bonariensis and very perennial.

Clematis heracleifolia 'Cassandra'
Shrubby, blue-flowered clematis with fragrant
flowers in autumn. 'Cassandra' is shorter than most
and less likely to loll about. Popular with bees
and butterflies. Dies back to nothing in winter, so
remove the fading stems in November.

Penstemon 'Andenken an Friedrich Hahn' AGM
In good summers many penstemons carry on
flowering until late, but this Swiss-bred variety is
always the last. It's hardier than many too. Popular
with bees.

Gaura lindheimeri AGM
Given a warm spot, this blush-white willowy plant
will still be in flower in November. Can be brittle in
the wind, though.

Hedera helix
English ivy enjoys a juvenile stage when it clings and
then an adult arborescent stage of woodier growth.
The latter bears November flowers that linger into
winter. On clement days these will attract flies and
bees. Berries follow. Best on an edge.

Dahlia 'The Bishop of Llandaff' AGM
Single and peony-flowered dahlias go on until the
first frosts, providing pollen and nectar to late-flying
pollinators. This has bright-red flowers and dark,
ferny foliage.

Salvia microphylla
These woodier salvias are hardy enough to survive
from year to year. The lipped flowers often come in
shades of red and various pinks. Still going strong in
November, this is often the last refuge for bees.

10 DAISIES

Their name is a corruption of 'day's eye', so these plants want a warm and light position. Many chase the sun, so site them carefully or you'll only see the backs of the flowers.

Helianthus 'Lemon Queen' AGM
A tall and substantial, clump-forming, lemon-yellow daisy with great charm. Each flower is studded with dark anthers and, given room to shine, this is one of the best border plants in August.

Eupatorium maculatum Atropurpureum group 'Riesenschirm' AGM
The obvious partner for 'Lemon Queen', flowering at the same time and reaching a similar height, but producing burgundy clouds of flowers on dark stems whorled with good foliage. Butterfly heaven.

Helenium 'Sahin's Early Flowerer' AGM
This hybrid helenium tolerates drier conditions than forms of *H. autumnale*, flowering sooner, from July onwards, and generously repeating in autumn. Each brown-coned flower is slightly different and the warm orange glow is dazzling. Good foliage too.

Aster × *frikartii* 'Monch' AGM
Probably the best aster ever bred and certainly the longest-flowering one, beginning in July and carrying on until late September. Long-rayed lavender daisies held above dark-green leaves. Drought tolerant, so no mildew!

Solidago rugosa 'Fireworks' AGM
A refined golden rod, with clear-yellow, arching heads of flower that attract flies and smaller hoverflies from August. The green buds add much to the border before it flowers.

Symphyotrichum 'Little Carlow' AGM
A small-flowered blue aster which bears sprays of flower in late summer. The buds always have a tinge of red and this upright plant is perfect on the corner of a border.

Rudbeckia laciniata 'Herbstsonne' AGM
A tall, willowy rudbeckia with clean yellow flowers, each with a green central cone, held way above the foliage. A partner for tall grasses.

Rudbeckia fulgida var. *deamii* AGM
Crisp yellow daisies centred in rich-brown, on a medium-high perennial with good green foliage. Begins in July and persists into autumn.

Anthemis 'E. C. Buxton' AGM
Lucid-yellow daisies are held on an upright plant with dark filigree foliage from summer onwards. Divide regularly to keep it vigorous – just pull shoots from the base and pot up.

Echinacea purpurea 'White Swan'
I raise my echinaceas from seed because most named forms are micro-propped and rarely come through winter. They flower in July and persist into late August, and I have seen territorial disputes between butterflies over them.

The feathery remains of *Stipa barbata*, a summer-flowering ostrich-feather grass twine through echinaceas

BIBLIOGRAPHY

Essential reading

Bourne, Val (2004), *The Natural Gardener*, Frances Lincoln, London

Early, Jeremy (2013), *My Side of the Fence*, Jeremy P. Early, Reigate

Golley, Mark (2007), *The Complete Garden Wildlife Book*, New Holland, London

Goode, David (2014), *Nature in Towns and Cities*, HarperCollins, London

Owen, Jennifer (1991), *The Ecology of a Garden: the First Fifteen Years*, Cambridge University Press, Cambridge

Owen, Jennifer (2010), *Wildlife of a Garden: a Thirty-year Study*, RHS, Wisley

Tait, Malcolm (ed.) (2006), *Wildlife Gardening for Everyone*, Think Publishing, London

Wilson, Ron (1979), *The Back Garden Wildlife Sanctuary Book*, Astragal Books

Informative websites

British Hedgehog Preservation Society: www.britishhedgehogs.org.uk

British Trust for Ornithology: www.bto.org

Buglife: www.buglife.org.uk

Bumblebee Conservation Trust: www.bumblebeeconservation.org.uk

Butterfly Conservation: www.butterfly-conservation.org

BWARS: www.bwars.com

Freshwater Habitats: www.freshwaterhabitats.org.uk

Froglife: www.froglife.org

Pesticides Action Network: www.pan-uk.org.uk

Plantlife: www.plantlife.org.uk

RSPB: www.rspb.org.uk

Wildlife Trusts: www.wildlifetrusts.org

Woodland Trust: www.woodlandtrust.org.uk

Bee books

Alford, D. V. (1975; reprint 2011), *Bumblebees*, Northern Bee Books, Hebden Bridge

Benton, Ted (2006), *Bumblebees*, HarperCollins, London

Edwards, Mike, and Jenner, Martin (2005), *Field Guide to the Bumblebees of Great Britain and Ireland*, Ocelli, Eastbourne

Falk, Steven (2015), *Field Guide to the Bees of Great Britain and Ireland*, British Wildlife Publishing, Totnes

Feltwell, John (2006), *Bumblebees*, Wildlife Matters, Battle

Goulson, Dave (2003), *Bumblebees: Their Behaviour and Ecology*, Oxford University Press, Oxford

Kirk, W. D. J., and Howse, F. N. (2012), *Plants for Bees*, International Bee Research Association, Groombridge

Prys-Jones, Oliver E., and Corbet, Sarah A. (2011), *Bumblebees*, Pelagic Publishing, Exeter

Pollination

Barth, Friedrich G. (1991), *Insects and Flowers: the Biology of a Partnership*, Princeton University Press, Princeton

Proctor, Michael, Yeo, Peter, and Lack, Andrew (1996), *The Natural History of Pollination*, HarperCollins, London

General insect books

Barnard, Peter C. (2011), *The Royal Entomological Society Book of British Insects*, Wiley-Blackwell, Oxford

Brock, Paul D. (2014), *A Comprehensive Guide to Insects of Britain and Ireland*, Pisces Publications, Totnes

Chinnery, Michael (2010), *Garden Pests of Britain and Europe*, A. & C. Black, London

Grissell, Eric (2001), *Insects and Gardens*, Timber Press, Maidenhead

Habitats

Peterken, George (2013), *Meadows*, British Wildlife Publishing, Totnes

Monographs

Hoverflies

Hall, Stuart U. A., and Morris, Roger (2016), *Britain's Hoverflies: a Field Guide*, Princeton University Press, Princeton

Stubbs, Alan E. (1996), *British Hoverflies: Second Supplement*, British Entomological and Natural History Society, Reading

Stubbs, Alan E. and Falk, Steven (1983), *British Hoverflies: an Illustrated Identification Guide*, British Entomological and Natural History Society, Reading

Lacewings

Plant, Colin W. (1997), *A Key to the Adults of British Lacewings and Their Allies*, Field Studies Council, Shrewsbury

Solitary wasps

Yeo, Peter F. and Corbet, Sarah A. (1995), *Solitary Wasps* (Naturalists' Handbooks 3), Richmond Publishing Company, Slough

Butterflies and moths

Newland, David, Still, Robert, and Swash, Andy (2013), *Britain's Day-Flying Moths*, Princeton University, Princeton

Oates, Matthew (2011), *Butterflies*, National Trust, Swindon

Thomas J. A. (2007), *Philip's Guide to Butterflies of Britain and Ireland*, Philip's, London

Beetles

Forsythe, Trevor G. (2000), *Ground Beetles* (Naturalists' Handbooks 8), Pelagic Publishing, Exeter

Hedgehogs

Morris, Pat (2006), *The New Hedgehog Book*, Whittet Books, Stansted

Morris, Pat (2014), *Hedgehogs*, Whittet Books, Stansted

Reeve, Nigel (1994), *Hedgehogs*, Poyser Natural History, London

Slugs and snails

Barker, G. M. (ed.) (2004), *Natural Enemies of Terrestrial Molluscs*, CABI Publishing, Wallingford

Cameron, Robert (2008), *Landsnails in the British Isles*, Field Studies Council, Telford

Rowson, Ben, *et al.* (2014), *Slugs of Britain and Ireland: Identification, Understanding and Control*, Field Studies Council, Telford

Ladybirds

Hawkins, Roger D. (2000) *Ladybirds of Surrey*, Surrey Wildlife Trust, Woking

Mann, Darren J. (2002), *Ladybirds: Natural Pest Control*, Osmia Publications, Sileby

Roy, Helen E., *et al.* (1989), *Ladybirds* (Naturalists' Handbooks 10), Pelagic Publishing, Exeter

Aphid predators and biological control

Davis, B. N. K. (1991) *Insects on Nettles* (Naturalists' Handbooks 1), Richmond Publishing Company, Slough

Helyer, Neil, Brown, Kevin, and Cattlin, Nigel D. (2003), *A Colour Handbook of Biological Control in Plant Protection*, Manson Publishing, London

Helyer, Neil, Cattlin, Nigel D., and Brown, Kevin (2014), *Biological Control in Plant Protection: a Colour Handbook*, Taylor and Francis, Abingdon

Malais, M. H., and Ravensberg, W. J. (2003), *Knowing and Recognizing: the Biology of Glasshouse Pests and Their Natural Enemies*, Reed Business Information, Doetinchem

Moreton, B. D. (1969), *Beneficial Insects and Mites*, Bulletin 20, HMSO, London

Rotheray, Graham E. (1989), *Aphid Predators* (Naturalists' Handbooks 11), Richmond Publishing Company, Slough

ACKNOWLEDGEMENTS

Most of all thank you to my Best Beloved who, as always, was enormously supportive. Better halves are the unsung heroes of publishing and he is a gem!

My great thanks also go to Marianne Majerus who photographed the garden on four occasions with great dedication – making it look better than it is!

I must also thank the brilliant designer, Ocky Murray, who worked so hard on this book. I am also indebted to Heather Robbins, who did the index for me. And thank you to Brenda Updegraff for her extraordinary editing skills – which are second to none.

Thank you to all the team at Kew Publishing, principally Gina Fullerlove for agreeing to do the book. Thanks also to Sara Redstone of Kew who read the first draft and was wildly enthusiastic. Thanks also to Lydia White, also of Kew, for all her help and finally, last but not least, huge thanks to Andrew Illes for making it happen!

ILLUSTRATION ACKNOWLEDGEMENTS

Val Bourne: title page, 4–5, 7 four pictures, 11 three pictures, 15, 16 two pictures, 19 four pictures, 20 two pictures, 22, 23, 26, 31, 34 right, 35 right, 47 four pictures, 59, 64, 67, 69 lower left lower right, 74, 75, 78 left, 79 both pictures, 80, 82, 84, 85, 86 left, 89, 95, 97, 100 left, 103, 105, 115, 118, 119, 121 right, 122 two pictures, 123 two pictures, 124, 126–7, 129, 130, 138, 140, 142, 144–5, 147, 148, 151, 153 three pictures, 157 four pictures, 161 two pictures, 162 right, 165 four pictures, 167, 168, 173, 175, 177, 180, 183, 184, 185, 195, 202, 204 three pictures, 207 both pictures, 211, 214, 223, 231, 232, 234, 235, 237, 241; BTO: 25 Edmund Fellows, 181 John Harding, 186–7 Jill Pakenham; Buglife: 135 Roger Key, 137, 168 right Roger Key, 199 Roger Key; Bumblebee Conservation: Trust, 34 left, 35 left, 154–5, Ben Darvill; Butterfly Conservation: 170 right Jim Asher; Steve Falk: 162, 204, 212, 215, 217, 218; Freshwater Habitats: 208–9 David Orchard; Gap, 12–13; Getty Images, 191; Marianne Majerus: title, 2, 9, 28–9, 33 both pictures, 36, 39, 40, 42-3, 45, 47, 48, 50, 53, 54-5, 57 two pictures, 60 two pictures, 61, 63, 68, 69 upper left and right, 70–71, 73, 76, 77, 78 right, 86 right, 88, 90–1, 93, 94, 96, 99, 100 right, 101 two pictures, 102, 104, 106, 108, 110–11, 113, 114, 116–17, 121 left, 141, 220–1, 224, 227, 229, 238, 245, 246, 251, 252; People's Trust for Endangered Species: page 188–9, Dave Bevan, 192 Dave Bevan, 196 Pam Lovesay.

Page numbers for illustrations are in **bold**

It's all hands on deck in spring - with lots to plant